AutoCAD for Theatrical Drafting

A Resource for Designers and Technical Directors

John Keisling

Routledge
Taylor & Francis Group

NEW YORK AND LONDON

First published 2021
by Routledge
605 Third Avenue, New York, NY 10158

and by Routledge
2 Park Square, Milton Park, Abingdon, Oxon, OX14 4RN

Routledge is an imprint of the Taylor & Francis Group, an informa business

Library of Congress Cataloging-in-Publication Data
Names: Keisling, John, author.
Title: AutoCAD for theatrical drafting : a resource for designers and technical directors / John Keisling.
Description: New York, NY : Routledge, 2021. | Includes bibliographical references and index.
Identifiers: LCCN 2020047329 (print) | LCCN 2020047330 (ebook) | ISBN 9781138578449 (hardback) | ISBN 9781138577763 (paperback) | ISBN 9781351264365 (ebook)
Subjects: LCSH: AutoCAD. | Theaters–Stage-setting and scenery–Design and construction–Computer programs. | Carpentry drafting–Computer programs.
Classification: LCC PN2091.S8 K37 2021 (print) | LCC PN2091.S8 (ebook) | DDC 620/.00420285536–dc23
LC record available at https://lccn.loc.gov/2020047329
LC ebook record available at https://lccn.loc.gov/2020047330

ISBN: 978-1-138-57844-9 (hbk)
ISBN: 978-1-138-57776-3 (pbk)
ISBN: 978-1-351-26436-5 (ebk)

Typeset in Myriad Pro
by KnowledgeWorks Global Ltd.

Contents

Acknowledgments   vi

Introduction   vii

1. Downloading AutoCAD®   1

2. A Review of Theatrical Drafting Practices   8

3. Exploring Model Space   14

4. Drafting 2D Shapes   30

5. Modifying 2D Shapes   41

6. Layer and Property Managers   53

7. Blocks and Block Editing   61

8. Creating Title Blocks and Reference Lines   67

9. A Brief Introduction to Dynamic Blocks   74

10. External References   83

11. Exploring Paper Space   91

12. Dimensions and Notations   100

13. Plotting and Publishing Sheet Layouts   109

14. Exploring 3D Model Space   112

15. 3D Modeling   121

16. Manipulating 3D Objects   128

17. Solid Editing   132

18. Plating 3D Models   143

19. Camera Views and Animation   155

20. AutoCAD for Production and Engineering   161

References   167

Index   168

Acknowledgments

Writing a text book is the one thing that I never thought I would do, but here I am, with my name on the cover. I would be remiss if I didn't acknowledge the people who helped to make this happen.

First and most importantly, I must thank my wife Margaret and the continued support and encouragement that she provided while I was writing this text. I could not have done this without you. You are an amazing wife and an even better mother to our four beautiful children.

I must also acknowledge my editor Lucia, who was always so patient with me throughout this process. Thank you so much for helping me get through this process and sticking with it. Thank you also to the technical editors who made so many great suggestions and the entire team at Routledge for all of the work in seeing this project through.

Thank you also to Robert Coleman, Jim Lile and Joshua Wickham, who convinced me to come to graduate school and each taught me so much. This book is only possible because of the influence you each have had in my life.

Thank you also to all of my colleagues and students who have supported the creation of this text over the past few years. I appreciate all of the work and dedication each of you show every day.

And finally, a thank you to my mother. You are an inspiration to me each and every day.

INTRODUCTION

What This Book Is Not

This book is in no way intended to be an all-inclusive book discussing all of the capabilities and commands available within AutoCAD. This book is also not intended to be a drafting book. While theatrical drafting practices are discussed within the text, it is recommended that students have an understanding of these practices prior to using this text. In my drafting courses, students complete hand drafting packages with paper and pencil and then I have them duplicate those drafting plates within AutoCAD using the commands and processes discussed in this text.

What This Book Is Intended to Be

The intent of this book is to pare down the commands in AutoCAD and only discuss how to use those that are most frequently used when completing drafting for theatrical productions. It is recommended that users follow along in the AutoCAD program, performing the steps for a command as they work their way through this text. While this text will only discuss individual commands, it is recommended that users of this text will combine many of the commands discussed into projects to complete drafting packets of objects and assemblies.

A Note about Lighting Design

While this text book does not specifically exclude the drafting of lighting designs and light plots, I have found throughout my career that most lighting designers prefer to use computer-aided design software other than AutoCAD. As a Technical Director, I also tend to be more focused on the engineering and construction of scenery. Because of these two factors, the drafting of lighting instruments and positions will only be briefly discussed in this text. The majority of the text covering the drafting of these items is used as an example on how to make and use dynamic blocks within AutoCAD.

A Note about Images

All images contained within this text are screen shots taken either directly from the AutoCAD software or contain material created by the author within the AutoCAD software.

Autodesk screen shots reprinted courtesy of Autodesk, Inc.

Autodesk, AutoCAD, DWG, the DWG logo and Inventor are registered trademarks or trademarks of Autodesk, Inc., and/or its subsidiaries and/or affiliates in the United States and other countries.

1

DOWNLOADING AUTOCAD®

The first step in learning to use AutoCAD is to navigate the process of downloading the software to your computer. When AutoCAD was first introduced, you would purchase a CD Rom or Floppy Disk and install the program to your computer. Now the software is downloaded and installed from the internet. This chapter will cover the different types of AutoCAD licenses that you can secure, the system requirements needed for your computer and walk you through the installation process all the way to opening the program.

AutoCAD vs. Cad for Mac

It is important to note that AutoCAD is a different program than CAD for Mac®. AutoCAD can only be run on a Windows® platform, and CAD for Mac is designed for a MAC/IOS® system. The two programs function in much the same way, however, CAD for Mac seems to lose some of the automated processes that help to speed up the drafting process, especially when it comes to laying out and plotting 3D drafting. CAD for Mac also has a drastically different user interface and lacks many features that CAD drafters rely on both for 2D and 3D drafting. If you work solely in CAD for Mac, learning to overcome these differences is fairly simple; however, transitioning between AutoCAD and CAD for Mac can be quite an undertaking. Since many Mac computers have the capability of running a Windows platform, I encourage my students to use the Windows version (AutoCAD) if at all possible.

AutoCAD Licenses

When you purchase AutoCAD you are actually purchasing a license, or a subscription, that allows you to use the program until that license expires. There are several different types of licenses available, and depending on your situation, one may be more appropriate than the others.

Perpetual License

Prior to 2016, Autodesk offered customers the ability to purchase a perpetual license that never needed renewal. The cost of this license was near $4,000. While it never needed to be renewed, it also did not allow users to update to a new version of the software without purchasing a new license. Autodesk has phased out perpetual licensing and now exclusively offers subscription licenses in their place.

Annual Subscription

An annual subscription allows you to download the most recent version of AutoCAD and use that subscription for one year. When you download the program, Autodesk will send you a product key and serial number that you will enter into the program. At the end of 12 months, the program will lock you out until you renew your subscription. At the time of the writing of this book, an annual subscription cost a little more than $1,600. You also have the choice to purchase a multi-year license.

Monthly Subscription

Similar to an annual subscription, a monthly subscription allows you to use the program for 30 days. At the end of 30 days, the program will lock you out until you renew your subscription. At $200 a month, the cost in the long run is significantly more than an annual subscription, but may be the right choice for someone working on a project in which they need only short-term access to the program. Autodesk now also offers a quarterly license, which will give you access for 90 days at a time.

Educational License

In an educational outreach effort, Autodesk has created an online educational community where students and those working in education have the ability to download free versions of several software programs produced by Autodesk, including AutoCAD.

According to the Autodesk website, to receive an educational license from Autodesk you must "attend or teach at a qualified institution or be licensing software on behalf of a qualified institution." You also must agree to use the program for educational purposes only.

Prior to downloading and installing educational software, you must first register for an account with Autodesk. When you sign up for an account on the Autodesk educational website, the positions that you can select from are: Student, Educator, IT Administrator for an educational institution and Student Design Competition Mentor. You must register your Autodesk account using an email address from an educational institution (ending in .edu). You will also be asked to provide verification of your educational standing by uploading a supporting document, such as a photo of your student ID. Once Autodesk has confirmed the verification documents, you will receive an email stating that you qualify for the educational license.

This license comes with two "seats" meaning that you can download the program onto two devices. You will have the choice of downloading the newest version of the program, or one of the previous three releases of the program.

The AutoCAD educational version is exactly the same program as the full version of AutoCAD with the exception that every drawing that you print will have an educational stamp stating "CREATED USING AN AUTODESK EDUCATIONAL PRODUCT." This will be true of any file that was modified in an educational version of the software, even if it is also manipulated or printed from a full version of the software.

System Requirements

AutoCAD is a large program with amazing capabilities. That means that it takes considerable computing space on your computer, especially if you plan to do any 3D modeling. As such, there are system requirements that your computer must have to be capable of downloading and running the program. These published requirements serve as a baseline for smaller scale 2D drafting and basic 3D modeling. There are also recommended settings, which help when doing larger files and 3D modeling. Even with the recommended settings, you may find that your computer may run slower at times, and the program may occasionally crash. It is important to be patient, save your work often, and run as few programs as possible in the background while using AutoCAD. System requirements for AutoCAD programs based on release year can be found on Autodesk's knowledge network (knowledge.autodesk.com). It is important to check your computer settings against these requirements before beginning the process of downloading the program.

To check your system specifications from a Windows 7 platform, click on the Start menu at the bottom left of your desktop and navigate to the Control Panel. From a Windows 10 platform, you will need to click on the Start menu and search for the Control Panel by typing "Control" into the search bar and selecting the Control Panel. With the Control Panel open click on "System" and a pop-up window will give you information about your operating system, your processor and your installed and available memory.

From a Mac machine, click on the Apple menu, and then click on "About This Mac." A window will load that provides you with information about your operating system, your processor and your installed and available memory.

A Note about Processors

Autodesk recommends a 64-bit operating system with 16 GB of memory for 3D modeling, and AutoCAD 2020 and later versions require a 64-bit operating system. AutoCAD 2019 and earlier versions can be installed on 32-bit operating systems. 32-bit operating systems can be capable of 3D modeling, especially considering the smaller size of theatrical drafting compared to the capabilities of AutoCAD. However, beginning in 2016, AutoCAD has relegated some of the tools for plotting 3D drawings to only be included on the software for 64-bit PCs. While this text will cover the work around for 32-bit machines and AutoCAD for Mac, the time savings with a 64-bit machine are unmatched.

Mouse Necessity

While laptop computers come equipped with track pads, a detached mouse with a scroll wheel is essential for drafting at reasonable speeds within AutoCAD. In order to speed up your drafting process, you will need to learn to use shortcuts and limit keystrokes, and the use of a detached mouse is significantly better at this than fumbling with a track pad.

Creating an Autodesk Account

Once you have created an Autodesk account, you will be able to select the program you wish to download and Autodesk will send you an email to the registered address that will include a product key and serial number to register your software.

To download the educational version of AutoCAD or AutoCAD for Mac, go to the following website: https://www.autodesk.com/education/free-software/all

AutoCAD

Architects, engineers, and designers rely on Autodesk® AutoC/ With AutoCAD, you get access to seamless workflows, specializ new automations to help you achieve the ultimate productivity powerhouse performance, visualize Xref changes, enhanced Bl version control to take your designs to the next level. Built for for the future.

System Requirements

Note: AutoCAD for Mac and Mac OS x 10.13 (High Sierra) compa
Get AutoCAD for Mac

Select the AutoCAD Icon, which will direct you to the page in Image 1.1. If you are using a Mac/IOS platform, select "Get AutoCAD for Mac" from this page.

From this page, you will be able to sign in to your Autodesk account, or create an account if you have not done so. Remember to receive the educational version of the program, you must register using an email address from an educational institution.

If you wish to purchase a full version of the software, visit the following site where you can download a 30-day trial. At the end of the trial, you will need to purchase a subscription license to continue using the program. The steps for downloading the program are nearly identical no matter which license you choose to use.

https://www.autodesk.com/products/autocad/overview

Downloading AutoCAD

Sign in to your Autodesk account and then select the version of AutoCAD (which release year) your operating system and your preferred language. Click on the "Install Now" button and then read and agree to the licensing agreement.

When the file appears, click **Open** to start the installation process.

Once you have made the appropriate selections, Autodesk will populate a serial number and product key on the above web page. Autodesk will also send this information to your registered email address. If you ever need to reinstall the program, this serial number and product key will allow you to do so without acquiring a new license.

Click on the red "INSTALL NOW" button. At this point, you will receive a pop-up window from Autodesk with the License and Services agreement. Once you have read the agreement, click the "I accept" button and then click the blue "Install" button. Doing this will begin the process of downloading the setup wizard for AutoCAD. You will need to save this wizard in a place that you can easily find (such as your desktop). Once you have selected a place to save the wizard to, a window will load (Image 1.2) informing you that your installation is downloading and the setup wizard will be located in the save location specified.

Double-click on the icon for the setup wizard and run the program. Click the run button and the program will begin downloading. If you receive an error message stating "something is preventing windows from running the program," this is almost always for one of two reasons:

1. Your computer does not have the necessary requirements to install this version of AutoCAD. If this is the case, you will need to install an available previous release for which your device meets the system requirements.
2. You already have a license to a previous version of AutoCAD with this login registration. While you do receive two seats, or the ability to download the program to two devices, you must download the same version of AutoCAD to both devices. When you renew your license, you will have the option at that time to update to a newer version or remain with your current version of the program. If this is the case, you will need to start the download process again selecting the version of AutoCAD that you have previously installed on a separate device.

Once the installation/download program has run its course, you will receive a window on your screen that will allow you to install certain tools that help if you are managing multiple AutoCAD licenses across several computers (such as in a CAD lab, etc.). Unless you are managing a computer lab, these tools are unnecessary and you should click the "Install Now" button on the right.

Finishing Installation

Once you have completed the process of installing AutoCAD to your computer, you will receive a couple of windows that will pop up on your screen. One is a window that includes articles and videos selected by the Autodesk team for instructional purposes. These articles change frequently, and can be a good way to keep up with recent updates in new releases of the software. This window will also inform you of any updates that Autodesk has released for your version of AutoCAD. Closing this window will load a window telling you that you have successfully installed the listed selected products. Clicking the "Launch Now" button will direct you to the opening screen for the program.

Migrating Custom Settings

If you have a previous version of AutoCAD installed on your system, a window will load that will allow you to "Migrate Custom Settings" into your new version of the program. As you will learn, AutoCAD is an extremely customizable program. The ability to migrate settings allows much of this customization to appear consistent when updating to a newer release of the software. Migrating settings is possible to do at any time, but if you have a previous version installed, migrating the recommended settings at this time will save time later. Make the selections you wish to import and proceed with finalizing the installation.

Registering Your License

At the completion of the installation, a dialog box will load asking you to activate your product license. You have 30 days after installation to activate the license or you will not be able to continue using the program. Click "Activate" to activate the license or "Run" to run the program and activate the license at a later time.

Opening AutoCAD

Once you have completed the process of installing, launching and registering the program, you will be taken to a window called Model Space where you can begin to draw and design. Clicking the small black x in the upper right corner will close this individual drawing and take you to the AutoCAD home screen, while clicking the larger red X just above this will close the entire program. When you open the program in the future (double-click the desktop icon to open), you will be taken to the AutoCAD home screen (Image 1.3) where you will be able to access all

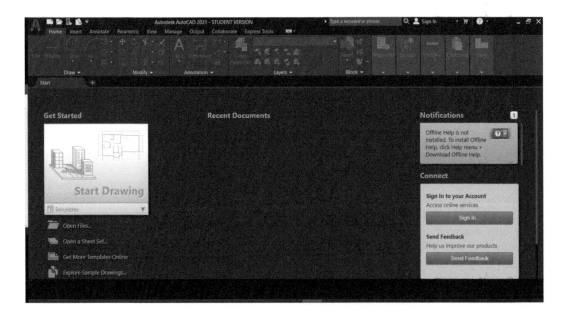

of your AutoCAD files. Following installation, it is a good idea to close the program, restart your computer, and then to reopen the program to ensure there were no errors with the installation.

Uninstalling and License Transferring

If you wish to uninstall an Autodesk program from your computer, you will need to use the "Uninstall Software" function from your computers utilities and settings. However, when you do this, the license for that software will stay attached to the device that the software was originally downloaded to. If you wish to transfer that license to a different computer, you will need to use the License Transfer Utility (LTU) included with your software.

If you are using a Windows platform, navigate to the Start menu and open the folder titled Autodesk. Open the folder with the program you wish to transfer the license of (i.e. "AutoCAD 2019") and click on the LTU. From a Mac OS platform, In the Finder, under applications, the LTU is in a folder with your product.

Once you have located and clicked on the LTU, sign in to your account and follow the step-by-step instructions as the LTU will walk you through how to transfer the license to a new machine.

2

A REVIEW OF THEATRICAL DRAFTING PRACTICES

As you may already know the acronym CAD stands for *Computer-Aided Design*. As wonderful as AutoCAD is for automating the process of design and drafting, paper layouts created within the software and then printed continue to be the primary means of communicating these designs.

In an effort to standardize drafting practices, the United States Institute of Theatre Technology (USITT) has released a document detailing standard theatrical drafting practices. Theatre artists, however, continue to be fiercely independent and often abandon these drafting standards in favor of a personalized drafting style. As an educator, I use the USITT drafting standards as a baseline to provide the new draftsperson with a sound foundation and then allow them to make changes to find their own personalized style.

Settings within AutoCAD allow us to automate the process of setting and easily repeating these standards and styles. Much of this is controlled by variables contained within style managers. These variables can be saved as part of a template file that allows you to set them a single time and use them for all future drafting. Paper sizes, title blocks, reference lines and much more can also be saved in these template files, preventing the need for a significant amount of repeated work each time you begin an AutoCAD file. As you progress through this text, these style managers will be introduced. As changes are made and styles are defined, it will be appropriate to update your template file with the new style definitions.

I recommend taking a hand drafting course prior to beginning the use of any CAD program to provide a firm foundation in laying out drafting plates. This book is not intended as a drafting text, but rather to teach how to use AutoCAD to complete theatrical drafting plates. However, this chapter will discuss recommendations for the styles that will be defined in the style managers based on the USITT defined drafting practices.

Paper Sizes

Paper comes in many sizes. Within theatrical drafting, there are several paper sizes that are acceptable, and what size you choose to use has to do with a lot of factors, including what you are drawing and at what scale, what the intended use of the drawing is and (when using a CAD program) what your printing capabilities are.

Table 2.1 Common Paper Sizes

Paper Size	Size in Inches	Typical Use
Letter	8.5×11	Individual elements and objects/drafts for estimates and sketches
Ledger	11×17	Some construction drawings
Arch D	24×36	Ground plans, center line sections, elevations, construction drafting, some light plots
Arch E	36×48	Some ground plans and center line sections and many light plots

While the list of available paper sizes is extensive, the following sizes are the most commonly used for theatrical drafting in the United States. Similar sizes are used internationally following recommendations by the International Organization for Standards (ISO). Whatever size is used, each individual sheet of paper is referred to as a drafting plate.

Title Blocks

Whatever paper size(s) you choose to use, each drafting plate should have a title block that includes important information regarding the drafting included on that plate. Title blocks can either be placed along the entire length of the right side of a page (Image 2.1) or a smaller title block can be placed in the bottom right-hand corner of the page (Image 2.2).

Each title block should contain the following information about the production:

Producing Organization   Designer's Name
Show Title
Director's Name   TD Name (ME for Light plots)

While the above information is consistent throughout a production, each title block should also contain the following information specific to the page that it is on:

Drawing Name   Scale of Drawing   Draftsperson
Plate Number   Plot Date   1st or 3rd Angle Projection

Note that for a plate with multiple drawings of different sizes and scales, it is appropriate to put "Scale as Noted" in the title block and then specify the scale for each individual drawing in a reference line. Also note that when working in the United States, declaring whether the drafting is using 1st or 3rd angle projection views in a title block is often omitted, because 3rd angle projections are the standard and therefore drafting is assumed to follow that methodology.

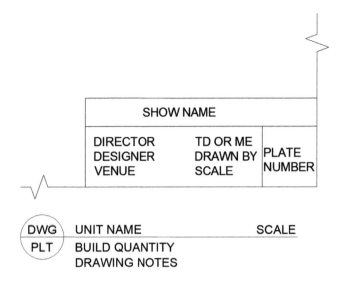

Reference Lines

A plate that only has one drawing on it, such as a ground plan, will have a title block that includes all information for that drafting. However, there are many times when a plate will include drafting for multiple objects and assemblies, and while the title block provides general information about that sheet, more detailed information such as material, build methods and specific notes are needed for individual drawings included on the sheet.

Reference lines are centered underneath individual drawings and include information specific to the individual drawing. Image 2.3 shows a typical reference line that includes the following information:

Drawing Number   Drawing Title   Scale of the Drafting

Plate Number   Build Quantity and Method   Drawing Specific Notes

Line Types and Line Weights

Line type refers to the type of line or the pattern a line follows. Is it a continuous unbroken line, a broken or dashed line, etc.? Line weight refers to the thickness of the line that is being drawn. In hand drafting, creating different line weights is accomplished by adding more or less pressure to the drawing utensil being used, or by changing between drawing utensils. In AutoCAD drafting, lines can be set to print at a specific thickness to provide a contrast in line weights.

Most draftspersons will use at least four line weights in their drafting: a very thin line, a thin line, a medium line and a heavy line. Table 2.2 contains a short list of common line types with their uses and suggested line weights for each use. It is also worth noting that many draftspersons define line weight in millimeters instead of inches. Settings within AutoCAD will allow you define line weights in either format.

Table 2.2 Common Line Types and Line Weights

Usage	Line Type	Line Weight
Objects	Solid	Thick 0.020″ (0.5 mm)
Title blocks	Solid	Extra thick 0.035″ (0.9 mm)
Reference lines	Solid	Thin 0.012″ (0.3 mm)
Dimensions and notes	Solid	Thin 0.012″ (0.3 mm)
Section lines	Phantom	Extra thick 0.035″ (0.9 mm)
Sectioned objects	Solid	Extra thick 0.035″ (0.9 mm)
Hatching	Solid (vary direction)	Very thin 0.006″ (0.15 mm)
Hidden objects	Hidden	Thin 0.012″ (0.3 mm)

Drawing Layouts

When several views of the same object are included in a drafting, they are placed in an orthographic layout. Orthographic projections are two-dimensional drawings used to describe or represent a three-dimensional object by drawing the individual sides of that three-dimensional object. Normally, three views (top, front and side) are sufficient to provide the information needed to communicate the details of an object. Orthographic layouts prescribe what positions are to be used when placing any of the six views of an object.

Hidden Lines

A hidden line is a line composed of short dashes. In an orthographic projection drawing, hidden lines are used to denote a feature that exists within the object(s) represented, but would not be visible from a particular view. For example, if an object had a feature on the left face that did not exist on the right face of the object, that feature would appear drawn in a hidden line on the right side projection view. It is standard to draw these hidden details in a thin line weight.

1st Angle vs. 3rd Angle Projection

It is helpful to know that there are two methods of laying out orthographic projection views depending on geography. The United States, United Kingdom and Australia generally use what is known as 3rd angle projection. In this method, you imagine unfolding a cube and placing the appropriate view of the side of an object on the side where that cube portion would unfold to. This means that the view of the right side of the cube would be placed on the right of the front view of the cube, with the matching corners closest to each other (Image 2.4).

Most of the remainder of the world uses the ISO standard 1st angle projection. In this method, it is helpful to imagine using the same cube, but instead of unfolding the cube, you would roll the cube on its side. Meaning that the image displaying the right side of the object would appear to the left of the image displaying the front side of the object, and so forth (Image 2.5).

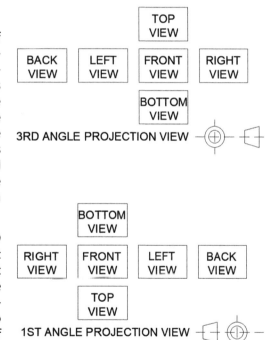

In the United States, 3rd angle projection is used nearly exclusively and a draftsperson who uses 1st angle projection is likely to have parts and assemblies built incorrectly. Whether you use 1st angle or 3rd angle projection, it is good practice to label it accordingly on your drafting plates, especially if you are working internationally. International symbols are used to denote which projection view is being used. Whether you are using 1st angle or 3rd angle projection, all views are always drawn to the same scale and should align with each other. The bottoms

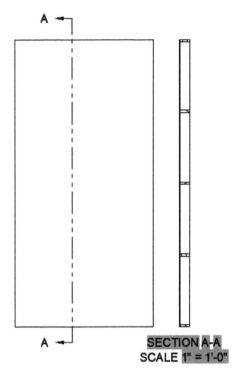

SECTION A-A
SCALE 1" = 1'-0"

of the object are placed along the same plane on the paper, as well as the vertical sides of the object aligning between top, bottom and side views.

Section Views

Sometimes it is helpful and/or necessary to provide a little more detail than would be included in a typical orthographic projection view. In theatrical drafting, this is particularly true when communicating details about molding, window mullions, trim heights of borders and electric battens and the like. When this need arises, a section view can be invaluable.

A section view allows you an imaginary look inside of an object or scenic element. Imagine cutting a flat in half and then turning half of it 90 degrees to see the inside. The line that you would cut the flat along would be your section line and the view you see when looking at the remaining half would be the section view (Image 2.6).

A center line section follows the same principles, but the imaginary cutting line would be the center line of the stage, displaying all scenery, lighting and masking accordingly.

Notice in the figure that the arrows at the ends of the section line point in the direction you are looking when viewing the section view. These arrows are labeled, here with an "A" on both ends. The section view is then labeled as Section A-A with the scale of the section. Section views can be scaled to a larger scale than the original orthographic view to provide clarity and greater detail when needed. Section views should be sequentially numbered throughout a drafting packet, with Section A-A being the first and then continuing to Section B-B, etc.

Below are the settings that I use when drafting section views in AutoCAD:

- Section lines are phantom line type with a line weight of 0.014"
- Object lines of objects cut by the section line are solid lines with a line weight of 0.014"
- Object lines of objects not cut by section line are solid lines with a line weight of 0.010"
- Objects cut by the section line are hatched with a line weight of 0.002"
  - Hatch lines are rotated for clarity when two cut objects appear next to each other

Annotation

This term refers to the dimensions and notations given within a drawing layout to help explain sizes and features of an object or assembly. It is important to ensure that your dimensions and notations are clear and concise, easily readable both in font type and size, and assembled in an organized manner.

There is an abundance of standards for dimensioning orthographic construction drawings. These standards become increasingly complex when dealing with precise parts that need to meet minimal allotted tolerances within thousandths of an inch to be accepted. Covering these types of standards would take an entire textbook. Geometrical dimensioning and tolerance (GD&T) is an art form, and there are many reference materials available that can lead you in the right direction if you wish to pursue this further. Within theatrical design and construction, outside of precision machine parts, we are typically less concerned with being this accurate, and usually accept scenic elements that are constructed within 1/16 of an inch of their design, eliminating the need for such specific dimensions and annotations.

The following are the settings that I use for annotation and dimension on 24 × 36 Arch D drafting plates. While these, certainly, are not the only options or acceptable methods in the field, I have found that these settings provide for clean and concise construction plates that are easy to read, and lead to fewer mistakes on the shop floor.

DIMENSION STYLE FOR 24 × 36 ARCH D CONSTRUCTION PLATES

- Use a 1/8″ break between the object and the extension line to delineate between the two
- Place 1/8″ filled arrows at both ends of the dimension lines
- Use Arial font at 1/8″ text height for dimension text
- Always give inches within dimensions (12′–0″ instead of 12′)
- Place the text of the dimension so that it can be read either from the bottom or the right side of the page
- Dimensions of angled cuts to be given to the nearest whole number of degrees, unless more precision is required (such as a 22.5 degree cut)
- Dimension any holes to be drilled with a diameter

ANNOTATION AND LEADER LINES FOR 24 × 36 ARCH D CONSTRUCTION PLATES

- Information for individual drawings should be given within reference lines
- General notes can be placed within the plate if the note applies to all drafting contained on the plate
- For very important notes, it is appropriate to use 1/4″ text height
- Leader lines can be used to bring attention to specific parts of an object and to provide further clarification
  - Leader Lines have 1/8″ closed filled arrow heads
  - Text is 1/8″ text height Arial font
  - Leader lines point to middle of first line
    - Alternately, leader lines can underline text of first line

3

EXPLORING MODEL SPACE

When you first open AutoCAD, you are taken to a start page that gives you several options for opening an AutoCAD drawing. On the left of the page there is a large "Start Drawing" option that will take you directly to a new clean drawing file. Below that option there are several other options for opening previously saved files and templates. Opening a previously saved file will open that file at the last point that it was saved. A template is a blank drawing with specific personalized settings. Later in this chapter, we will discuss how to save a template with preferred user settings to avoid the need to choose these settings each time you begin a new drawing.

In the middle of the start page is a list of Recent Documents. These are the most recent AutoCAD files that you have been working on. As you save AutoCAD files to your device, this will fill in with shortcuts to those files. On the right of the start page are notifications about new AutoCAD features as well as a box that allows you to sign in and connect to your Autodesk account.

To begin your first AutoCAD drawing, click the Start Drawing option at the top left of the start page. This will open a drawing file entitled Drawing 1.

Model Tab vs. Layout Tab

While there is a lot to look at when you first open an AutoCAD drawing, it is best to break it down and look at the individual parts and options within the drawing file. While there are many places to start, we will first delineate between the Model tab and the Layout tabs. These are located at the bottom left of the window and are labeled Model, Layout 1 and Layout 2. You can switch between these tabs by clicking on them.

Model Space

Clicking on the Model tab takes you to a window called Model Space. The entire area in the middle of the screen is the Model Space. This space is infinite in size and can be seen by zooming and panning around the screen. Within Model Space you are able to draw objects at their actual size. This is a little difficult to understand at first as a large object can be viewed all at once within your screen. However, thinking of objects that are drawn within Model Space as being drawn at their full size helps to understand the difference between Model Space and the Layout tabs. In Model Space, users can draw and modify objects using commands, shortcuts and customizable panel buttons that surround the drawing area.

The drawing area operates on an X, Y, Z axis, with the X axis going from left to right on your screen, the Y axis going from top to bottom on your screen and the Z axis going from out to in on your screen. Only the X and Y axes are used for two-dimensional drafting, while the Z axis is used for 3D modeling.

Within the drawing area are a couple of small toolbars that tell you what view you are looking at within the drawing, as well as what visual style you are drafting in. These toolbars and the View Cube that is at the top right of the drawing area will be discussed as part of 3D modeling. For two-dimensional drafting, the view should be set in the default top view and the visual style should be set to the default 2D Wireframe visual style.

You can zoom in and out of a drawing by using the scroll wheel on your mouse. Upon installing the software, moving the scroll wheel up will zoom in, or magnify objects on the screen, while moving the scroll wheel down will zoom out. Additionally, you can pan around the screen by holding the scroll wheel down and moving your mouse.

The Command Line

At the bottom center of the Model Space window is a rectangular box called the Command Line (Image 3.2). While this is somewhat of an over-simplification of the process, AutoCAD inherently works by entering commands into the Command Line, and then completing the drafting operations associated with those commands on your screen. The Command Line can be moved around the screen and placed wherever is preferred for an individual user, including placing it on a secondary screen. The Command Line can also be "docked" to one edge of the screen. To move the Command Line, click on the small dots on the left side and drag it around the screen with your mouse.

Layout Tabs

Layout tabs are the spaces that are designed to create custom paper space layouts. You can add and delete Layout tabs so that each drafting plate has its own Layout tab. You can also rename Layout tabs to make their names more descriptive of what is contained within each layout.

Layout tabs are discussed at length in Chapter 11 of this text. At this point, it is enough to know that within the Layout tabs you can create windows that look into Model Space and set your Model Space drawings to specific scales within your drafting plates.

AutoCAD Menu and Quick Access Toolbar

At the top left corner of your AutoCAD screen is the distinctive AutoCAD letter A. Clicking on this A will load the AutoCAD menu where you can open and save files, import and export files, plot and publish drafting and view and manage drawing utilities. Many of the items within this menu will be discussed throughout this book.

Next to the AutoCAD menu is the Quick Access toolbar (Image 3.3). This toolbar also allows you to open and save drawing files, as well as plotting drafting. The Quick Access toolbar also contains an Undo and Redo button. At the right side of the Quick Access toolbar is an arrow that loads a slide-out menu that allows you to customize what objects are shown on the Quick Access toolbar.

Function Bar

For the remainder of this chapter, we will explore the basic settings within Model Space. All of these are customizable based on your individual preferences. Some have simple on/off functionality and some have many options to choose from. We will begin discussing these settings with the Function Bar, which is located in the bottom right-hand corner of the AutoCAD drawing.

The Function Bar controls many settings that determine how Auto-CAD reacts to your drafting style. Many of these settings not only have a button on this toolbar, but also have a shortcut within your Function keys on your computer keyboard (i.e. F1, F2, etc.) that toggle these options on and off. The Function Bar appears differently in a Layout tab than it does in Model Space. The organization of the Function Bar is also customizable using the Customization button

located on the right end of the Function Bar. Image 3.4 shows the Function Bar as it appears within Model Space when you first install the software. Hovering your mouse over buttons on the Function Bar will load the name of the tool as well as the keyboard shortcut for using those tools.

Help Menu

While there is no button for the Help menu on the Function Bar, the shortcut to access the AutoCAD Help menu is the F1 key. Pressing F1 will load the AutoCAD Help menu which is quite extensive. When you first open the Help menu, there are several general options as well as sub-options under each option. Many of these include videos walking you through steps to do basic AutoCAD functions. The Help menu also gives you the opportunity to connect with the Autodesk community where there are many forums with people willing to answer more difficult questions that may not be included in the answers on the Help menu.

Model Space Selection

To the far left of the Function Bar is the word Model. This is a way to ensure that you are drawing in Model Space. Clicking on the word Model will cause AutoCAD to navigate to a Layout tab. If you are in a Layout tab and click on the word Paper, AutoCAD will take you to a Model Space window within that Layout tab. You will need to click on the Model tab at the bottom left of the AutoCAD window to navigate back to Model Space.

Grid and Grid Snap

Directly next to the Model selection button within the Function Bar is the "Display Drawing Grid" button (F7). When you first open a new AutoCAD drawing, a grid is displayed in the drawing window. You can set this drawing grid to be of specific sizes once you have set your drawing units for a particular drawing file. Selecting this button or its shortcut will toggle the visibility of this drawing grid on and off. With this button and all other buttons on the Function Bar, the button will highlight when it is toggled on and the highlighting will turn off leaving a greyed out button when it is toggled off.

The next button is the Snap Mode button (F9). Within AutoCAD, you can designate default locations that you want to repeatedly select with your cursor while drawing. These default locations are called snap points. Turning on the Snap Mode adds each point of your drawing grid to your snap points. It is important to know that the Snap Mode button can be activated even if the drawing grid is not displayed.

As a Technical Director, I almost always have both of these settings turned off. Having them turned on can cause you to accidentally snap to a point of the grid instead of a location on a drawing object that is close to that grid snap point. However, some draftspersons find that the Snap Mode can be helpful when the grid is set to specific distances.

Orthogonal and Polar Snap Modes

The next two selections on the Function Bar are the Ortho Mode (F8) and Polar Tracking (F10). You can select one or the other of these, or neither, but you cannot have both options toggled on at the same time.

Turning on the Ortho Mode restricts your cursor to 90 degree angles, meaning that you can draw only in 90 degree angles unless you manually override the functionality by entering specific angles at specific times within commands or by selecting snap points on existing geometry. Turning on the Polar Snap mode allows you to restrict your cursor to specific angles other than 90 degrees. Selecting the arrow next to the Polar Tracking button allows you to select which angles you wish to use from a prescribed list.

The Drafting Setting dialog box (Image 3.5) will allow you to input custom polar tracking angles that are not listed in the default list. To access this toolbox, click on the arrow next to the Polar Tracking button and click on "Tracking Settings." Alternately, you can type the command DS

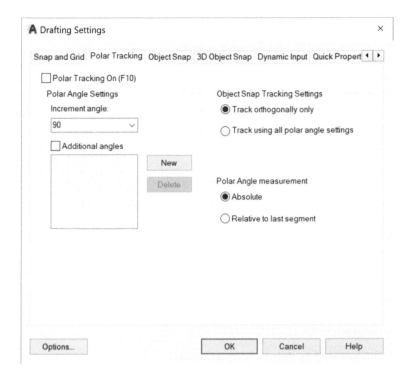

into the Command Line and press Enter to load the Drafting Settings dialog box. This box will also allow you to set the spacing of your drawing grid, if you choose to use one, as well as to define other drafting settings, such as which geometric snap points you prefer to use.

Isometric Drafting

Selecting this button turns the drawing space to a 30 degree angle allowing the user to draw 2D isometric views of objects more easily. As this book will cover 3D modeling and how to project isometric views from a 3D AutoCAD model, it is not necessary to cover the use of this function other than to point out to the user that this exists as an option for those wishing to make 2D isometric views without out creating a 3D model. Selecting the arrow next to the button will load a menu that allows you to select which view you wish to draw the isometric view from and F5 allows you to toggle between the three options available.

Object Snap and Object Snap Tracking

The next button on the Function Bar is the Object Snap Tracking (F11). Next to this is the Object Snap button (F3) that allows your cursor to default to snapping to locations on previously created geometry. You can define which snap locations you wish to use by opening the drop-down menu next to the Object Snap button on the Function Bar, or by using the Drafting Settings dialog box. Personally I have chosen the following default object snaps:

| Endpoint | Center of Circle | Intersection of Objects |
| Midpoint | Quadrant of Circles | Insertion Point of Objects |

There is also a function within AutoCAD called Osnap Override. When using a drafting command and before clicking on a geometric snapping point, you can hold the Shift button and right-click on your mouse to load the Osnap Override list. This will allow you to select from a list of geometric object snaps to define which one you wish to click on. AutoCAD will ignore all other snap points until you have clicked on the screen to choose the snap point you have defined.

The Object Snap Tracking (F11) option allows you to hover over a default object snap and then track your cursor at a predefined angle away from that point. This can be helpful as it allows you to snap to imaginary intersection points that extend beyond existing geometry.

Annotation Tools

The Annotation tools on the Function Bar allow you to input dimensions and notations into Model Space and then to define the scale that the model will be printed so that the annotations print at appropriate sizes. While it is helpful to know that these tools are available, the industry standard is to input dimensions and notations into a paper space layout, eliminating the need to use these Annotation tools.

Workspace Settings

The gear icon on the Function Bar allows you to switch between Workspace settings. Workspace settings organize commands and user preferences based on what type of work you are doing. 2D drafting tools are prioritized in the Drafting and Annotation Workspace setting, while 3D modeling tools are prioritized in the 3D Modeling and 3D Basics workspaces. As this book will begin with covering 2D drafting and annotation, set the workspace setting to Drafting and Annotation for the time being. Saving a customized workspace will be discussed at the end of this chapter.

Dynamic Input

The remainder of the Function Bar options are not turned on when you first install AutoCAD. While there are over 30 options available, this text will cover only a few of them. To load an option to the Function Bar click on the three bars at the right end of the tool bar, and then scroll to and click on the option you wish to add. You can also remove objects from the Function Bar in the same method.

Turning on Dynamic Input (F12) puts a rectangular box next to your cursor that shows you the command that you are currently entering and using within the drawing file. Some users prefer having the Dynamic Input turned on as it provides real-time information about the commands they are using directly next to the objects they are working with. With some commands, it also allows you to quickly input information (such as dimensions) associated with the commands. Other users find that it duplicates information that already exists within the Command Line and prefer to leave this function turned off.

Selection Cycling

This button allows you to toggle on and off the Selection Cycling within the AutoCAD drawing window. When there are multiple objects drawn on top of or close to each other, having the Selection Cycling turned on will load a drop-down menu that will allow you to select which of the objects that you wish to select instead of always selecting the top most object.

3D Object Snap

Similar to the 2D Object Snap option, the 3DOSnap function (F4) allows you to select a series of default snap points on 3D objects. The arrow next to the button will load a drop-down list that allows you to select which points you wish to use as default snap locations. These may also be set using the Drafting Settings toolbox.

Line Weight Display

This button allows you to choose whether or not to show line weights on your computer screen. Line weights can be set to print whether or not they are shown on your computer screen.

Transparency

When drawing 3D objects, you can add a function of transparency. This can be helpful when drawing objects like acrylic sheet that has a transparent view to it. Showing transparency in AutoCAD takes up more computing space, so this option allows you to toggle the transparency off to save computing power.

Hardware Acceleration

The final button on the Function Bar that we will discuss is Hardware Acceleration. Oftentimes, the easiest way to boost performance and responsiveness in your drafting is to disable the Hardware Acceleration option. This may seem counter-intuitive, but Hardware Acceleration is meant to make video animations and camera views of 3D modeling clearer and sharper. Sharper imaging is not a necessity when drafting, and turning off Hardware Acceleration will allow your computer to follow commands more quickly without needing to fully render every object in high detail. The Hardware Acceleration button is listed as "Graphics Performance" when you click on the customization button at the right end of the Function bar.

And Much More

To this point, we have covered less than half of the nearly 30 options available on the Function Bar to customize the way AutoCAD works for you as an individual. The settings covered to this point in the book are perhaps the most important settings to know about as you begin learning the software, but as you gain experience, you may find that other settings contained within the Function Bar allow you to create a user interface that you find better adapts to your drafting. It will be helpful to familiarize yourself with these options and return and experiment with them to make the best customization of the program for you as an individual.

Using Drafting Commands

If you click within the AutoCAD window and begin typing, whatever you type will appear in the Command Line. Each function that AutoCAD is capable of performing has a specific command and keyboard shortcut. Typing these commands into the Command Line tells Auto-CAD which command you wish to perform next, or which option you wish to choose when you have options within a given command. The Command Line will prompt you with the options that are available within each command.

If you have the Dynamic Input selection from the Function Bar turned on, your Command Line will extend into your Dynamic Input and the commands that you enter with your keyboard and the options available within those commands will appear next to your cursor as well as in the Command Line.

The most effective way to improve drafting speed within AutoCAD is through the use of keyboard shortcuts to enter commands. The use of these shortcuts can reduce keystrokes, which in turn, reduces drafting time.

To begin using a command using keyboard shortcuts, type the keyboard shortcut into the Command Line and press Enter. The Spacebar also acts as a secondary Enter button within AutoCAD and the two are interchangeable. It is also possible to set your mouse settings so that right-clicking on the mouse also duplicates the Enter button. Follow the prompts provided in the Command Line and press Enter again (Spacebar/right-click) to complete the command. At any point while using a command, pressing the Escape button on your keyboard will exit and abandon the command.

The Ribbon

At the top of the drawing screen is a pallet of buttons that provide access to selected commands within AutoCAD. This pallet is called the Ribbon.

As with most things in AutoCAD you can customize the view of the Ribbon, or even turn it completely off. To turn the Ribbon off, type RIBBONCLOSE into the Command Line and press Enter. To turn it back on, type RIBBON into the Command Line and press Enter. At the top right of the Ribbon, next to the word Performance there is a small drop-down window. Selecting this menu will allow you to select from a list of options that will change the look of the Ribbon from minimized panel buttons to showing the entire Ribbon on your home screen. All of the functionality of the Ribbon exists no matter which view is chosen. While minimizing the Ribbon increases the size of the drawing area, it also adds a step to selecting commands from the Ribbon.

Clicking on a button within the Ribbon will instigate the command associated with that button. Each of these commands also has a keyboard shortcut. If you hover your cursor over a button without clicking on it, a short description of that command will appear in a window. Continuing to hover over that button for a few more seconds will expand the description to include an example of how that particular command works.

The Menu Bar

Similar to the Menu Bar in word processing programs, AutoCAD also has a Menu Bar. Once again, this can be turned on and off depending on personal preferences. To toggle the Menu Bar on and off, type MENUBAR into the Command Line and press Enter. A subcommand option will appear in your Command Line. Typing 1 and pressing Enter will turn the Menu Bar on and typing 0 and pressing Enter will turn the Menu Bar off.

Some of the functionality in the Ribbon is duplicated within the Menu Bar; however, it also holds shortcuts to other customizable settings within AutoCAD, as well as having the ability to save and open AutoCAD files. Functions from both the Ribbon and the Menu Bar will be discussed throughout this text.

Setting Drawing Units

When you first open an AutoCAD drawing, AutoCAD reads and measures in unspecified units. You must define these units before you begin drafting in order to specify dimensions of objects. That function is accessed through the Drawing Utilities tab of the AutoCAD menu (the A in the top left corner). You can also access this option by typing UNITS into the Command Line and pressing Enter. Either method will take you to the Drawing Units toolbox. Here you can set your drawing units. To get drawings in feet and inches, select Architectural. You can also select the precision of the drawing. Most theatrical drafting uses 1/16" precision. On the right you can set your angle type as well (decimal degrees) and select a precision for that as well. You also should select the insertion scale (inches) and, if you wish, the units to specify lighting intensity (usually not necessary for theatrical drafting).

Setting the drawing units allows you to create geometry to a specified dimension. Adding dimensions to that geometry is a separate process and until you specify units for dimensions you will not be able to accurately dimension drawn objects. You can, however, measure distances using the Measure command on the Ribbon, or using the Distance (DI) command as a keyboard shortcut.

Options

Much of the visual customization available within the drawing area of AutoCAD is contained within the Options dialog box. To access this dialog box, navigate to the AutoCAD menu in the top left corner of the screen and click on the Options selection box at the bottom right of the menu next to the Exit AutoCAD selection box. Alternately, you can type OPTIONS into the Command Line and press Enter.

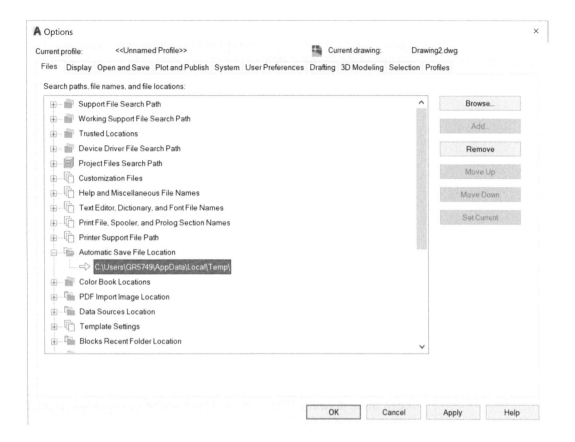

Files

Within the Options dialog box are several tabs. Each of these tabs holds their own options for customizing the look and functionality of Auto-CAD. The first tab is the Files tab. This tab has a lot of information specifying the save locations of AutoCAD files.

Here, you can specify the location in which you wish AutoCAD to save Automatic Save files. You do this by selecting the plus sign next to the Automatic Save File Location, loading the drop-down menu. Click on the save file location so that it is highlighted. (This is a default save location that often does not exist on your machine, and needs to be changed accordingly.) Once the save file location is highlighted, select the Browse button on the right hand of the screen and navigate to the new save file location.

The File menu also will allow you access to mapping template and plot style table locations, both of which will be covered at later points in this text.

Display

The Display tab allows a lot of changes in the appearance of the program. The top left section is titled Window Elements and offers a lot of customization through selection boxes. Here, you can customize the look of the Ribbon and how long it takes for Ribbon tips to appear.

Under the top heading of Color Scheme you can select a dark or light color scheme. This choice affects the color scheme of AutoCAD not including the drawing area.

To change the colors of the drawing areas select the "Colors" selection box within the Window Elements section. When you do this, a Drawing Windows Colors dialog box appears. On the left are several context options such as 2D Model Space, Sheet/Layout, etc. Select the drawing area you wish to change the color of and on the right select the Color drop-down box and choose the color you wish to use for your drawing area background. While many colors are available, black or white are the most commonly used to allow other colors to be used for delineating between objects.

Within the Display tab you can customize much of the visual appearance of AutoCAD. The crosshair size slider allows you to set how long the crosshairs of your cursor are as a percentage of the drawing area.

Open and Save

The Open and Save tab of the Options menu allows you to designate which file type you will use to save your drawings. I recommend saving AutoCAD drawings as older versions of AutoCAD drawings. For example, while using AutoCAD 2021, I save all of my files as AutoCAD 2013 drawings. This allows others with older versions of the program to open these drawings. The process of back saving can, however, result in larger drawing files.

Within the Open and Save tab you also specify how often AutoCAD automatically saves your drawing. It is easy to get caught up in drafting and forget to manually save your file. Having the ability for AutoCAD to automatically save your files prevents a lot of rework. These files will save with an AC$file extension in the location that you specified in the File tab of the Options toolbox. To open these files, select the file and manually overwrite the AC$files extension with a DWG file extension. This is done by highlighting the AC$file extension and typing "DWG" overtop of it. This will turn this file into a DWG file format that is able to be opened within AutoCAD.

If you are working from a Windows machine, often it will be set up to not show file extensions of files saved to your computer. To change this setting, click on your computer's Start menu and type Folder Options into the Search menu and press Enter. This will load a File Explorer Options toolbox to your computer screen. Click on the View tab, scroll down and uncheck Hide Extensions for Known File types.

User Preferences

Within the User Preferences tab you have the option to customize what happens when you use the right-click button on your mouse. There are two schools of thought on this. One school of thought is that right-click should always mean that you want to repeat the last command or to mean Enter if you are currently using a command. The second school of thought is that right-click should always load the Shortcut menu and should never be customized. I personally use a time sensitive right-click that I have found to be a happy middle ground between the two. As with many things within the program, this is customizable based on user preference.

To set your right-click settings, select the Right-Click Customization selection box which will bring up the corresponding toolbox.

The settings I use for right-click customization are as follows:

Default Mode	Edit Mode	Command Mode
Repeat Last Command	Shortcut Menu	Enter

Once these are selected, I also select "Turn on Time Sensitive Right-Click" which allows a quick right-click to always mean the same thing as pressing Enter, and a slightly longer right-click to follow the above guidelines.

Drafting

In the Drafting tab you can select the sizes for your auto snap markers as well as the aperture size. The auto snap markers denote points on geometry that you can select as a snapping point when drafting. The aperture is the rectangle at the center of the cross hairs on your cursor and the size of the aperture effects how close you need to be to select an auto snap marker or other object when drafting.

Selection

Within the Selection tab you can set the size of the pick boxes and grips on objects using the sliders at the top of the toolbox. Clicking on the Grip Color button allows you to choose what color the grips will appear in at different points of their use.

On the left side of the toolbox in the Selection tab is a button tiled Noun/Verb selection. In AutoCAD it is typical that we first enter into a command and then select what object we wish to perform that command with. This is called the Verb/Noun method of drafting. We are stating what we want to do (the verb) and then telling AutoCAD what object we want it to perform on (the Noun). Checking the Noun/Verb box allows you to work backward, first defining the object you wish to modify and then entering the command. When the button is turned on, you can work in either direction, but with the button turned off, you must enter the command (the verb) before selecting the object being modified.

At the bottom right corner of the Selection tab is an area titled "Preview." This setting allows you to customize what objects are highlighted on your screen at what times. If all the boxes are checked, then AutoCAD will highlight objects as you scroll over those objects with your mouse. You can filter when these preview highlights happen. Personally, I have unchecked "When no command is active" to prevent AutoCAD from highlighting any objects when I am not currently using a command. You can also filter out objects so that they are never highlighted. To filter objects, click on the "Visual Effect Settings" button located under the "Preview" area of the dialog box. A new dialog box will pop up allowing you to filter out such things as text, hatching, objects on locked layers, etc. so that they are never highlighted.

This Visual Effect Settings toolbox will also allow you to customize the color of crossing and selection windows (discussed further in later chapters) and to change the transparency of these windows.

Saving a Custom User Interface

When opening a new AutoCAD drawing, the program will default to previous settings that you have chosen in the Options tool box. However, if you change to a different workspace setting (such as 3D Modeling) when you change back to the Drafting and Annotation workspace, AutoCAD will forget much of the custom user interface that you have enabled and revert back to the original Drafting and Annotation workspace. This means that you will lose any toolbars that you have added or moved around the screen, as well as any changes that you have made to the Ribbon or the Menu Bar. Other customizable user settings will also revert to their defaults, including which options of the Function Bar are activated.

To save your customizations, it is good practice to save a Custom User Interface file (CUI). The simplest method to do this is to click on the arrow next to the gear icon in the Function Bar at the bottom right-hand corner of your screen. Click on "Save Workspace As" which will load a dialog box that will allow you to name and save the workspace in its current format.

These workspace settings can also be saved as CUIx files on your computer or on an external hard drive (such as a thumb drive). Saving a CUIx file on an external hard drive will allow you to load that workspace setting into an AutoCAD drawing. This can be especially useful if you are working in a space, such as a computer lab, where you are not the only one using AutoCAD on a specific machine.

To save a CUI externally, type the command CUI into the Command Line and press Enter. This will load the Custom User Interface toolbox (Image 3.8). Click on the Transfer tab at the top of the toolbox. On the left side of the toolbox, click on the plus sign to expand the "Workspaces" options. Click and drag your saved custom user interface from the left side of the toolbox and place it next to the word "Workspaces" on the right side of the tool box under the label "Customizations in New File." When you have transferred all of the custom workspaces you wish to transfer, click on the disk icon at the top right of the toolbox next to the words "New File" and save the CUIx file to a thumb drive. The workspace settings can be imported using the reverse method of dragging a saved file from the right side of the screen to the left side of the screen to be used in the current drawing.

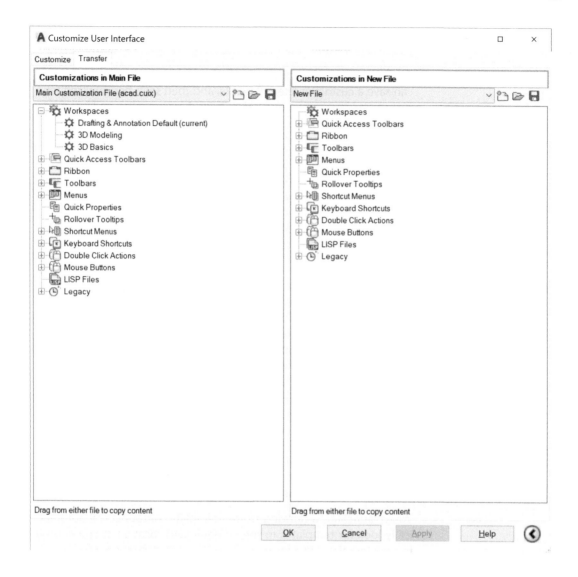

Saving a Drawing Template

As you progress through your learning of AutoCAD, it will be appropriate to save template files. Template files are AutoCAD files saved with a .dwt file extension that maintain styles, settings and layouts across drawing files. Template files maintain layer and property information, style manager settings, Layout tabs, previously created title blocks, and even print and plot settings. Many theatres have a template that includes geometry for their performance spaces already drawn within Model Space.

Beginning a new drawing from a template can save you a lot of time and unnecessary duplication of work. AutoCAD comes preloaded with several basic template files. To view the list of available templates that come with your AutoCAD installation, click on the AutoCAD menu (the A in the top left corner of the screen), hover over "NEW" and then click on "Drawing." You will be directed to a file manager page that allows you to select a template to use when beginning a new drawing.

Once you have information that you plan to use across drawings, you can save a customized template file, and then set a personalized template to be used when using the Quick Access toolbar to load a new AutoCAD file.

To save a drawing as an AutoCAD template, click on the AutoCAD menu in the top left corner of your screen, hover over the "Save As" button and then click on "Template" on the fly out menu on the right. A file manager window will load that defaults to the save location of the template files that came installed with your software. Name your template file, map the preferred save location if you wish it to be in a different location and click save. The file will be saved with a .dwt file extension.

To set a favorite or most used drawing template to be the default template used when opening a new file, you will need to go to the Options menu and define that. Type OPTIONS into the Command Line and press Enter, or navigate to the AutoCAD menu in the top left corner of the screen and click the "Options" button. Navigate to the Files tab at the top of the toolbox. In the main window of the toolbox, click on the plus sign next to "Template Settings" and then click on the plus sign next to "Default Template File Name for QNEW." Click on the file below this option (when you first install AutoCAD the default is "None"). With the file name highlighted, click the Browse button on the right side of the toolbox, navigate to the template you wish to use as your default in the file manager, and click Open. The word "None" will now be replaced by the file and extension for your chosen template. Click the "OK" button at the bottom of the toolbox to complete the selection.

When launching a drawing from a template, AutoCAD will automatically look for templates in their default save location. If you choose to save templates in a location other than the default save location, it is helpful to map that location, so that AutoCAD will look in your preferred save location when opening new drawings. To do this, navigate to the Options menu and click on the "Files" tab at the top of the tool box. Click the plus sign next to "Template Settings" in the main window and then click on the plus sign next to "Drawing Template File Location." Click on the file save location below this option so that it is highlighted. With the save location highlighted, click on the Browse button on the right side of the toolbox. Use the file manager window to navigate to the save location of your templates and click Open. This will update the location in the toolbox. Click OK at the bottom of the toolbox to complete this setting.

Opening vs. Loading Templates

It is important to delineate the difference between opening a template file and launching a new file based on a template. Using the "QNEW" tool in the Quick Access toolbar or the "NEW" tool from the AutoCAD, Start menu will launch a new file using the settings saved in the chosen template. This will allow you to create a new drawing that contains all of the settings specified in your template drawing. This will allow you to save this file as a new DWG file.

Using the "OPEN" tool in the AutoCAD Start menu or the "Open Files" tool on the AutoCAD, start page will open your template file. This will allow you to make changes to the base template file. Any changes that are saved during this process will overwrite your template file and those changes will be reflected at all future times when you load a file based on that template file.

4
DRAFTING 2D SHAPES

To open a new drawing, double-click on the AutoCAD application shortcut from your computer. If you will be using AutoCAD extensively, pinning the shortcut to the bottom of your computers home screen may be a good idea. From the AutoCAD start page, you will have access to the AutoCAD menu (the large A in the top left corner of the screen) as well as the Quick Access toolbar. To start a new drawing, click on the AutoCAD menu and click "New." AutoCAD will navigate to the location you have defined where you save your template files. Select the template file you wish to use and click "Open." AutoCAD will open a new DWG file on your screen with all of the template settings applied. If you mapped your QNEW settings in the Options menu, you can alternately click on the "New" button on the Quick Access toolbar, and AutoCAD will open a new DWG file from the template you have defined.

In this chapter, we will cover the process of drafting two-dimensional objects, such as polylines and circles. As you enter each of these commands, you will find that there are many options that are available within the commands. Keeping an eye on the Command Line will help as you begin learning the program. The Command Line will prompt you for the next step in the command as well as giving you options for keyboard entries to select from several options.

Entering Drafting Commands

As you draft, there are several ways to enter commands. In this chapter, we will be discussing drawing new objects. To draw a new object, you will need to tell AutoCAD which type of object you wish to draw, and then specify where on the screen and at what size you wish to draw that object. Each of the commands covered in this chapter has a corresponding button on the AutoCAD Ribbon. To begin a command, you can either enter the command or its shortcut via a keyboard entry in the Command Line and press Enter, or you can click on the corresponding button within the Ribbon. If you are using the keyboard to enter commands, it is helpful to remember that the Spacebar doubles as an Enter key, as does the right-click button of your mouse if you have chosen to set up your right- click settings to do so.

To the far left side of the Ribbon on the Home tab is the Draw panel (Image 4.1). This is where the Ribbon selection buttons are located for the commands covered in this chapter. Keyboard shortcut commands are called out in parentheses next to the command name throughout this chapter.

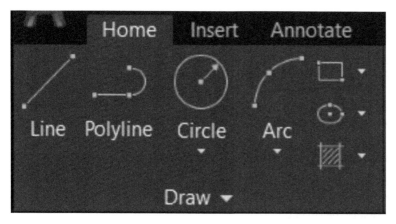

Line (L)

By definition, a line is a straight narrow mark between two points. Selecting the Line command allows you to draw a series of line segments by selecting points within Model Space. To begin, select the Line command on the Ribbon or use the keyboard shortcut to enter the Line command. The Command Line will now give you a prompt stating "Specify first point." Center the cross hairs of your mouse cursor on the screen at a point you would like to begin drawing your line and left-click to select that point as the start point for your line.

After selecting the first point, the Command Line will prompt you to select the next line point. If you click anywhere else on the screen, AutoCAD will draw a line to the second point that you have clicked.

Once you do this, the Command Line will prompt you to select the next point, and the next point, and so on. Each following point of the line can be drawn in any direction on the screen. This will continue until you escape out of the Line command. To escape from a command, press the Escape or Enter button on your keyboard.

Lines of Specified Dimensions

Often, you will find that you wish to specify the length of a line rather than clicking two points on the screen. To do this, enter the Line command and choose the start point of the line you wish to draw. Before clicking to define the second point of the line, drag your mouse cursor in the direction in which you wish to draw your line. While your cursor is hovering in that direction, type the length for the line you wish to draw into the Command Line and then press Enter. This will draw a line at the dimension that you specified in the direction that your mouse is hovering. If you have selected to restrict your cursor in either Ortho or Polar mode on the Function Bar, then your line will draw to the angles that you have specified within those modes.

Specifying Object Dimensions

When you enter dimensions into the Command Line for drawing objects, AutoCAD defaults to read those dimensions as units. When using Architectural units in a drawing, those units are converted to inches. If you wish to draw a line that is 3 feet in length, you would enter 36 into the Command Line for 36 inches. Alternately, you can override this default by typing an apostrophe (') into the Command Line to specify a dimension as feet instead of inches. To draw a line that is 3 and half feet in length, you could either enter 42 to specify inches or 3'6. Unless your units are set to architectural, AutoCAD will reject the apostrophe and not accept your dimension input.

To enter fractions of an inch, you have the option to use decimal equivalents following your inches or to hyphenate your dimension so that it would read either 3'6.5 or 3'6-1/2. Failing to hyphenate between the inch and the fraction would cause AutoCAD to read that measurement as 3 feet and 61 halves of an inch.

Object Selection and Object Grips

Once you have an object drawn on the screen, there are several ways to select the object. Selecting an object will allow you to modify, move or delete the object.

The simplest way to select an object is to center the crosshair of your cursor over the object and left- click on the object. You can select several objects this way by clicking on each object you wish to select. If you wish to remove an object from the current selection group, hold the shift button on your keyboard and left-click on the selected object. If you wish to deselect all objects selected, press the Escape button.

There are four ways to select multiple objects at once: two types of selection windows, one device called a Lasso and a selection method called a Fence.

Crossing Selection

A Crossing Selection, or a left crossing window, is a green selection window that will select all objects that the window intersects. To create a Crossing Selection, point your cursor in a blank section of the drawing area on your screen, quickly left-click the mouse and release the mouse button. This will create the start of the selection window. Drag your mouse to the left to the point where you wish to end the selection window and click to define the end point. All objects that intersect that window or are enclosed within that window will be selected.

Window Selection

A Window Selection, or a right crossing window, is a blue selection window that will select only objects that are completely enclosed within the window. It is created in the same manner as a Crossing Selection, but instead of dragging your cursor to the left, you drag it to the right to create a blue window. Any object that intersects the window but is not completely inside of the window will be excluded from the object selection.

The Lasso

When creating a selection window, holding the left-click button instead of quickly clicking and releasing it will create a selection device called a Lasso. A Lasso is a non-rectangular selection window that can be drawn in ameba-like shapes with your cursor. Drawing a Lasso to the left will create a Crossing Selection, selecting all shapes that intersect the window, and drawing a Lasso to the right will create a Window Selection that selects all objects completely enclosed within the Lasso.

The Fence

When using a command that requires you to select objects, AutoCAD will allow you to use a Fence selection to define what objects you wish to select. A Fence selection allows you to draw a line on your screen, selecting any objects that intersect with that line. To use the Fence command, enter a command (such as the Erase (E) command) type F for Fence into your Command Line or Dynamic Input and press Enter. Draw the Fence that intersects with all objects you wish to modify. Press Enter once to show a preview of what objects will be modified. Press Enter a second time to accept the modifications, or press Escape to exit the command.

Object Grips

When an object is selected, a set of small blue boxes appear on the object. These are called Object Grips. Each Object Grip allows you to stretch or otherwise modify the selected object. Modification of objects will be covered in Chapter 5.

Command Line Prompts

As you begin drawing objects, the Command Line will prompt you for the information the software is looking for in the next step of the command. Options to be used within a command (or subcommands) are provided as prompts in the Command Line. Typing the highlighted letters into the Command Line and pressing Enter will enter you into the chosen subcommand. You can also use subcommands by clicking on the name of the subcommand in the Command Line.

Polyline (PL)

Using the Line command creates individual line segments that are not geometrically connected and can be manipulated individually. Using the Polyline command creates line segments that are geometrically considered part of the same object.

Specifying Polyline Dimensions

Similar to a line, you can specify the length of each segment of the polyline by entering specified dimensions into the Command Line before selecting the next point of the polyline.

Including an Arc within a Polyline

While the method for drawing arcs is detailed below, that same method can be used to include an arc as a segment of the polyline by choosing the Arc subcommand within the Polyline command. Prior to selecting the next point on the polyline, enter the Arc subcommand and follow the prompts to include an arc.

Closing a Polyline

After selecting the second point of a polyline, a subcommand for Close will appear in the Command Line. Using the Close subcommand will cause the next point of the polyline to be drawn to the start point of the polyline, creating a closed polyline.

Undoing Polyline Segments

Using the Undo subcommand within the Polyline command will erase the last segment of the polyline that was drawn. This allows you to go backward within the command and make corrections without the need to delete your work and start again from the beginning. Once you have completed the Polyline command, using the Undo (U) command will undo the entirety of the polyline.

Width and Half Width

The Width and Half Width subcommands are options to specify how thick a polyline is drawn. Most users ignore these options and set the line widths manually or within the Layer Properties menu or within their Plot Styles (covered in Chapter 6).

Circle (C)

There are several options available within the Circle command to specify how a circle is drawn. These include defining the center point and the radius or diameter of the circle, specifying two points along the diameter of the circle, specifying three points along the tangent of a circle and specifying two points of the perimeter of the circle along with a radius. Whichever method is chosen, a circle is always drawn as a complete 360° closed circle.

Center Point and Radius

The default method to draw a circle in AutoCAD is to select the center point of the circle and then to specify the radius or diameter of the circle. After entering the Circle command, point the cross hairs of your cursor to the point where you wish to locate the center of your circle and left-click to select that point. You can now drag your cursor away from the center point and click on the screen to select the outer edge of the circle. Alternately, you can enter specified dimensions into the Command Line to specify the radius of the circle. To specify the diameter instead of the radius, enter the Diameter subcommand before entering a dimension.

Three-Point Method

To use the three-point method for drawing a circle, enter the Circle command by selecting the Ribbon button or entering the shortcut into the Command Line and pressing Enter. Prior to selecting the center point of the circle, enter the 3P subcommand. You will now be prompted to select three points along the perimeter of the circle you wish to draw.

Two-Point Method

Using the two-point method for drawing a circle allows you to draw the two end points of the circle's diameter. A circle will be drawn with the center point of the circle at the center point of the diameter you have specified.

Tangent, Tangent, Radius

This option allows you to select two points on the perimeter of the circle and then to specify the radius of that circle. This is a far less used method of drawing a circle, and can often lead to an error message if it is not possible to draw a circle that will state "Circle does not exist."

Arc (A)

This command allows you several options to draw an arc. Clicking the arrow below the Arc command on the Ribbon will load a number of options for drawing an arc. This section will cover only a few of the most commonly used methods for drawing an arc. Whichever method you choose to use, it is important to know that AutoCAD defaults to drawing most arcs in a counterclockwise direction.

Three-Point Method

The default method for drawing an arc is the three-point method. After entering the Arc command, click on screen to define the start point of the arc, click a second point along the length of the arc and then click the end point of the arc. The radius and length of the arc are thus defined by these three points. A three-point arc can be drawn in either a clockwise or counterclockwise direction.

Start, Center, End

This method allows you to select the end of the arc, then select the center of the arc's radius, and finally select the end point of the arc. To access this option, you can either click on the button on the Arc drop down menu on the Ribbon or you can use the subcommand options in the Command Line.

Start, End, Radius

This option is similar to the Start, Center, End method above, but changes the order in which points are selected. Here you select the start point of the arc, followed by the end point of the arc and finally define the radius of the arc. Once again, you can select this option from the drop down menu in the Ribbon, or by following the prompts in the Command Line.

Start, Center, Length

While less commonly used than the above methods, it is important to note that this option for drawing an arc can be misleading. Using this option allows you to specify the start point followed by the center point of the arc. Finally, it asks you for the length of the arc. What it is asking for is not actually the arc length, but rather the linear distance between the start and end points of the arc.

Repeat Last Command

When not performing a command, pressing the Enter button on your keyboard (or using the Spacebar or right-click settings) will repeat the most recently used command. However, it will not repeat the subcommands that you used. When drawing an arc, repeating the last command will enter you into the default for drawing an arc, but you will have to choose any subcommands that you wish to use that vary from the default. This is true of subcommands throughout the program.

Rectangle (REC)

The Rectangle command is perhaps the most used command when drafting theatrical scenery. Lumber, sheet goods and mechanical tubing are all rectangular in their two-dimensional shapes, requiring this command to be used repetitively in each drafting session. Drawing rectangles in AutoCAD is a fairly simple task, but as with many other commands, there are several subcommands that allow you to more fully define the finished look of the rectangle.

Default Method

The default method for drawing a rectangle is to specify opposite diagonal corners of the rectangle you wish to draw. Enter the command, select the first corner of the rectangle by clicking on the screen, and then specify the diagonally opposite corner to draw a rectangle.

Specifying Dimensions for Rectangles

The most common way to draw a rectangle is to specify the dimensions of the rectangle that you wish to draw. In order to draw a rectangle with specified dimensions, begin the Rectangle command by entering the shortcut into the Command Line or by selecting the button from the Ribbon.

Begin by specifying the first corner of the rectangle. Before selecting the opposite corner, enter D for dimension in the command options and press Enter, or click on the Dimension subcommand. When you do this, the Command Line will prompt you to enter the length for the rectangle. The length of the rectangle is always along the X axis of the screen and the width of the rectangle is along the Y axis of the screen. Enter the length of the rectangle and press Enter, then enter the width of the rectangle and press Enter.

After entering the dimensions of the rectangle, AutoCAD will ask you to specify the other corner point of the rectangle. You have defined the start point of the rectangle and the dimensions, and now AutoCAD is asking in which quadrant you want this rectangle to be drawn.

If you are drafting with the Dynamic Input function turned on in your Function Bar (F12), you can type the dimensions for your rectangle into the boxes included next to your cursor. To define the dimensions of the rectangle in this manner, enter the Rectangle command and click on your screen to choose your starting point. Drag your cursor diagonally away from your starting point in the direction that you wish to draw the rectangle. Two dimensions will appear on your Dynamic Input line. The dimension to the left is the X dimension and the one to the right is the Y dimension. With the X dimension highlighted, type the new dimension for the horizontal length of the rectangle. Press the Tab button on your keyboard to highlight the Y dimension and set the vertical height of the rectangle and press Enter to accept the dimensions and complete the rectangle.

Chamfer and Fillet

When you first enter the Rectangle command before selecting the start point of the rectangle you are given the option to chamfer or fillet the rectangle. A chamfer will put an angle across each of the corners of the rectangle, while a fillet will round the corners of the rectangle. Both of these functions can also be completed after the rectangle has been drawn through object modification (covered in Chapter 5).

When you select the use of a chamfer or fillet while drawing a rectangle, the Command Line will prompt you to specify the dimensions of the chamfer or the radius of the fillet. Entering a fillet or chamfer in a Rectangle command will cause that feature to appear as a default in all rectangles that you draw thereafter until you re-enter a chamfer or fillet of 0.

Drawing in Shapes

It is a good practice to draw objects as 2D shapes, such as circles, rectangles, polygons and closed polylines. As building materials are always a defined shape, this practice ensures that drawings created within AutoCAD can be realized on the shop floor.

This practice will also make the transition to 3D AutoCAD drafting significantly easier as two-dimensional closed shapes can be converted to 3D objects.

Polygon (POL)

A polygon is defined as a shape with three or more sides in which each side has an equal dimension. The Polygon command in AutoCAD uses the center of the polygon as a definition point for drawing a polygon. As such, it may help to draw a circle of a specified dimension to assist in the drawing of a polygon.

To begin the Polygon command, enter the shortcut in the Command Line or select the Polygon button on the Ribbon, which is located in a drop down menu next to the Rectangle command. When you enter the Polygon command, the Command Line will prompt you to select the number of sides for your polygon. Here you can enter any number greater than two.

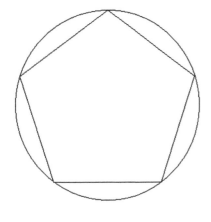

Once you have specified the number of sides to your polygon, you will need to specify the geometric center of the polygon. This is the point at which having a pre-drawn circle begins to help as you can now select the center point of the circle.

Once you have selected the center point of your polygon, you will need to tell AutoCAD whether you want to draw the polygon inscribed within the circle (Image 4.2) or circumscribed about the circle (Image 4.3). Once you select which side of the circle you wish to draw the polygon on, you will need to select the radius of the circle. If you have pre-drawn a circle, you can click the edge of the circle. If you do not have a circle drawn, you can enter the radius dimension into the Command Line and press Enter.

Ellipse (EL)

As with other drawing tools within AutoCAD, the Ellipse tool has options for the methods used to draw this object.

Center

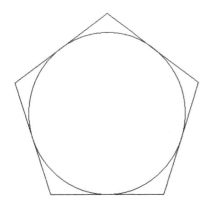

The default mode for drawing an ellipse is to specify the center of the ellipse and then to specify the end point of one axis, followed by the end point of the second axis. As with other tools, you can either click a point on the screen to specify the end point of each axis or type dimensions into the Command Line to specify the distance from the center of the ellipse to the end point of each axis.

Axis, End

This method of drawing an ellipse allows you to specify the entire length of one axis and then to specify the distance from the center of the first axis to the edge of the second axis.

Construction Line (XL)

Most of the panels on the Ribbon have an arrow at the bottom of the panel. Clicking on this arrow will load a slide out that contains more tools associated with that Ribbon panel. In the slide out of the Draw tab on the Ribbon, there are several drawing tools. One of these tools is the Construction Line. A Construction Line is a line that extends to infinity in two directions across your screen. These lines can be used as reference lines for aligning objects on your screen (such as aligning orthographic views within Model Space), or can be used as boundaries for modifying objects.

When you enter the command for drawing a construction line, you are given a series of prompts in the Command Line for options within the command. From these options, you can choose to draw a horizontal or vertical construction line, or specify a different angle at which you would like to draw your construction line. Alternately, you can click two points on the screen to define the angle of the construction line.

Hatch (H)

The Hatch command allows you to draw a hatching pattern within a predefined closed object, such as a circle, closed polyline, rectangle or polygon. When you enter the Hatch command, the Hatch Creation tab (Image 4.4) will appear on the Ribbon.

Within the Hatch Creation tab, you can specify the objects to be hatched, the pattern of the hatching including standards from the American National Standards Institute (ANSI) for hatching, the spacing, angle and transparency of the hatching as well as the origin point of the hatching. The Hatch Creation tab of the Ribbon is fairly intuitive to use and allows you to quickly set the visual look of hatching within your drawing.

To modify and change the appearance of existing hatching, double-click on a previously drawn hatched object, and the Hatch Creation tab will reload in the Ribbon, allowing for adjustment.

All hatching selected in the original selection will be treated as an individual hatch creation, and changes or modification to the hatch will affect all objects hatched at that time. This makes it necessary at times to create separate hatching drawings for objects to allow variations in the direction of hatching of tangential objects.

Other Drawing Tools

In the slide out under the Draw panel on the Ribbon (in the same location as the Construction Line tool) are other less used drawing tools. Some of these tools will be covered as a part of drafting 3D objects while others will not be covered in this book as they are not commonly used for drafting in theatre. It is, however, recommended that you familiarize yourself with their location and basic functions as they may be useful in specific situations. As with other tools, the prompts in the Command Line will guide you through the options included in each of these tools.

Zoom (Z)

While not a command for drafting new objects, the Zoom command allows you to view objects on your screen. The scroll wheel on your mouse allows you to zoom in and out of the drawing space.

The command ZOOMWHEEL will allow you to change which direction the mouse wheel uses to zoom in and out of the drawing. When you enter the command and press Enter, the Command Line will ask you to "Enter a new Value for ZOOMWHEEL." The default of 0 will cause scrolling up with the mouse wheel to zoom in and scrolling down to zoom out. Changing this value to 1 will flip this orientation.

The Zoom command allows you to specify what you want to zoom to within your drawing. Several subcommands are provided allowing you to specify where you wish to zoom to within the drawing window. The Extents subcommand will zoom to the extreme edges of your drawing showing all geometry that exists within Model Space. Double-clicking the scroll wheel of your mouse will also cause AutoCAD to zoom to the extents of the drawing.

Regenerate (RE)

As you scroll and pan around the drawing window, occasionally, Auto-CAD will fail to fully render the geometry. This may cause circles to look less circular, intersecting lines to appear to have a gap between them, or to cause other geometric anomalies. While the software's memory recognizes this geometry as existing as it was entered, the visual effect may appear differently. Using the Regenerate command causes the drawing to refresh and for geometry to be rendered anew based on the current pan and zoom location within the drawing window.

5
MODIFYING 2D SHAPES

Perhaps the biggest benefit to using a computer-aided drafting program, such as AutoCAD, rather than traditional hand drafting is the ability to quickly modify, change and delete previously created geometry.

In this chapter, we will cover basic commands for modifying and changing the 2D objects that were covered in Chapter 4. Once again each of these commands has a selection button on the Ribbon. They are located on the Modify panel directly to the right of the Draw panel covered in Chapter 4 (Image 5.1). To begin a command, you may click the corresponding button on the Ribbon or use keyboard shortcuts. Additionally, if you have turned on the Noun/Verb settings, you can modify objects by first selecting the object and then selecting the command to modify the selected objects. Keyboard shortcuts are called out in parentheses next to the commands throughout this chapter. It is helpful once again to remember that the Spacebar doubles as an Enter button on your keyboard, as does the right-click button on your mouse if you have chosen that setting. Subcommands will appear and can be selected either by typing the highlighted letters and pressing Enter or by clicking on them with your mouse.

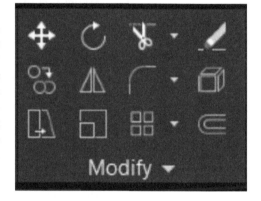

Stretching Objects with Grips

When you select an object, a series of blue boxes will appear on the object. These objects are called grips and can be used to modify the sizes and locations of objects drawn in Model Space. The number and location of grips change depending on the object selected. A rectangle and other closed polylines will have grips on each corner and the midpoint of each side, while a circle or arc will have a grip on each quadrant as well as their center points. Different grips will behave differently, but each will allow you to modify the size or location of objects. Multiple grips can be selected and edited at one time by holding down the Shift key on your keyboard as you select them.

Center Grips

Center grips appear on objects that have a center point and at least one radius, such as circles arcs and ellipses. A quick left-click on a center grip will attach that point to the center of your mouse cursor. You can then change the location of the object by clicking another location on the screen. Alternately, if you have your Polar or Orthographic modes turned on in your Function Bar, you can hover your mouse in the direction you wish to move the object, type the distance you wish to move the object into the Command Line and press Enter.

Edge Grips

Edge grips appear on the edges of objects, such as the midpoint between two corners of a polyline and on each of the four quadrants of a circle. Edge grips allow you to stretch the geometry of an object, making the radius of a circle larger, or extending one side of a polyline. Edge grips work in a similar fashion to center grips in that you can either click the desired destination of the grip or type a dimension to stretch that particular grip a defined distance.

Corner Grips

Corner grips appear at the corners of polylines and polygons, and allow you to change the geometry of the object by stretching that particular corner point to a new point on the screen. They operate in the same manner as other grips in AutoCAD.

Stretch (S)

There is a Stretch command with a corresponding Ribbon button. Entering the command will allow you to complete the same steps that you can complete with grips.

Move (M)

The Move command allows you to move a previously drawn object to a new location on your screen. To enter the Move command, type the shortcut into the keyboard and press Enter or select the Move button from the Ribbon. Once you have entered the command, the Command Line will prompt you for the next steps.

Begin by selecting the object(s) you wish to move. Note that all objects selected will be required to move in the same distance and direction. You can either select individual objects by pointing and clicking or select objects with object selection windows. Once all objects that you wish to move have been selected, press Enter to signal to the program that you have completed your selection.

Next, the program will ask you to specify a base point. You may select any object snap point, or an empty point on the screen as your base point. Specifying object snap points is helpful when you want to move a particular point of an object to a specific point on another object, while choosing an empty point on the screen is helpful if you wish to move an object a specified distance.

Once you have selected your base point, you will need to specify the destination point. You can either click a point on the screen (including an object snap point) or hover your mouse in the direction you wish to move the object and type the desired distance that you wish to move the object and press Enter.

Shortcut Menu

The Move command is one of the commands that appears on the AutoCAD Shortcut menu.

To move objects using the Shortcut menu, first select the objects you wish to move. After all objects that you wish to move are selected, load the Shortcut menu with a right-click on your mouse. Select Move from the Shortcut menu and then follow the prompts in the Command Line to select a base point and a destination point.

Copy (CO or CP)

This command works much the same way as the Move command, however instead of only moving an object, it makes a copy of the original object or group of objects selected and moves the copy to a specified point on the screen, leaving the original object in place.

Enter the command by either clicking the button on the Ribbon or typing the shortcut into the Command Line and pressing Enter. Select the object(s) you wish to copy, specify a base point and specify a destination point.

You may also select the objects first and use the Shortcut menu to copy the selection in much the same way you can use the Shortcut menu to move objects.

Mirror (MI)

The Mirror command will create a mirror image of an object or selection of objects about a plane defined by the user.

To enter the command, either use the Ribbon button or type the shortcut into the Command Line and press Enter. Select the objects you want to create mirror images of. Once all objects are selected, press Enter to signal that you have completed the object selection process.

Next, you will need to define the mirror plane. To do this, click two points on the screen with your mouse. The objects that you have mirrored are drawn as mirror images exactly the same distance from and on the opposite side of the mirror plane you have defined. As with defining base points for moving and copying, the points for the mirror plane can be selected as object snap points or as blank points on the drawing screen.

Once you have defined the mirror plane, AutoCAD will ask you whether or not you wish to erase the original objects. The default is to not erase objects, so if you wish to keep both objects, press Enter. If you wish to only keep the newly drawn mirrored object, type Y into the Command Line before pressing Enter.

Rotate (RO)

The Rotate command allows you to rotate an object about a defined center point. The center point can be defined as any point within the drawing window, whether it is a blank point in space, a point on another object or a point on or within the object(s) you are rotating.

To enter the command, either select the button from the Ribbon or type the shortcut into the Command Line and press Enter. Select the object(s) you wish to rotate and press Enter to signal that you have completed your object selection.

The Command Line will ask you to specify a base point. The base point for rotation is the center point at which you wish to rotate all selected objects about. Left-click on the point you wish to use for your rotational axis.

After selecting the base point, you will need to specify the rotation angle. You can either type an angle measurement into the Command Line and press Enter or you can use your mouse cursor to specify the rotation angle. If you have your Polar or Orthographic modes turned on in your Function Bar, AutoCAD will default to rotate objects to the angles specified within these settings.

Copy and Rotate

Within the Rotate command, there is an option to copy the selection being rotated. This will rotate the object as specified and leave a copy of the object in its original location. To accomplish this, select the Copy subcommand in the Command Line after selecting the base point but before defining the rotation angle.

Using Reference Angles

Along with the subcommand to copy a rotating object is a subcommand to use a reference point to define the rotation angle. To do this, select the Reference subcommand after selecting the base point but prior to defining the rotation angle.

The most common way to use the Reference subcommand is to select a reference angle beginning with the center point of the rotation and then selecting a point along the object you wish to rotate. Then you will select the new angle by clicking on the screen for a new rotation angle. The center point will remain the same.

Using Copy and Reference Angles

If you wish to both copy a rotating object and use a reference angle to define the rotation, you must choose the Copy subcommand first. After choosing the Copy command, AutoCAD will allow you to then choose the subcommand for using a reference angle.

Shortcut Menu

Similar to the Move and Copy commands, the Rotate command is also available on the right-click Shortcut menu. Select the objects you wish to rotate, right-click to load the Shortcut menu, and then select Rotate. Complete the remaining steps as listed above starting with selecting a base point.

Erase (E)

While there is a Ribbon button for erasing objects, as well as a keyboard shortcut (E), perhaps the simplest way to erase or delete objects from the drawing screen is to select the object you wish to erase and press the Delete button on your keyboard.

Undo and Redo

There is an Undo button on the Quick Access toolbar that will allow you to undo the previous command. The keyboard shortcut for Undo is U. You also have the option of using the Windows shortcut of holding down the CTRL button and pressing Z to undo the most recent commands.

The Quick Access toolbar also has a Redo command if you realize that you didn't actually want to undo the command you just undid. There is no keyboard shortcut for Redo, but you can type the entire command REDO into the Command Line to use this command.

The Undo tool will undo the previous command, and then the next previous command, and so on.

The command OOPS will undo the last Erase command without undoing any other commands, bringing back objects that were previously deleted.

Trim (TR) and Extend (EX)

The Trim command allows you to "cut" objects to a specified cutting plane, while the Extend command allows you to extend lines to a specified cutting plane. If you are in one command, you can switch to the other by holding the Shift button on your keyboard. As long as you hold the Shift button, AutoCAD will switch you to the command opposite of the one you selected, and will revert back to the selected command when you release the button.

To enter the Trim (or Extend) commands, select the button on the Ribbon, or type the keyboard shortcut into the Command Line and press Enter. Note that the Ribbon button for this command defaults to the last command that you entered (either Trim or Extend). If you wish to select the opposite command, click the drop-down arrow next to the Ribbon button where both commands will appear.

After entering the command, AutoCAD will prompt you to select your cutting edge. You can either select objects to use as your cutting edge or choose the default to use all objects as cutting edges. The cutting edges are the edges that objects will either trim or extend to within the command.

Erase and Undo

Within the Trim and Extend command, there are several subcommands. Two of these are the Erase and Undo subcommands.

Using the Erase subcommand allows you to erase the next object selected instead of trimming or extending that object. The Undo subcommand allows you to individually undo the last object trimmed or extended within the command. If you exit the Trim or Extend command and then use the Undo command all objects trimmed or extended during that command will be undone.

Join (J)

The Join command joins multiple adjacent objects into a single object. This command can be extremely helpful to create closed polylines from multiple objects.

To complete the Join command, enter the command by selecting the Ribbon button, or entering the shortcut into the Command Line and pressing Enter. Select the objects you wish to join and press Enter. Alternately, if you have enabled the Noun/Verb setting in the Options menu, you can select the objects first and then type the command into the Command Line and press Enter.

2D Polyline Selection (PEDIT)

The command PEDIT will also allow you to change a polyline after it has been created. Within the PEDIT command, subcommands will allow you to close a polyline, drawing a line from the two open ends of an existing polyline, or to open a closed polyline. You can also use the subcommand Join to add line segments or arcs to the open end of a polyline. Other sub commands allow you to control the width of the polyline, as well as to control the behavior of vertexes and curves contained within the polyline.

Overkill (OV)

The Join command requires objects to be connected end to end without overlapping each other. If the ends aren't perfectly touching, or if lines of the object are drawn on the same plane on top of one another, you will receive an error message in the Command Line stating that the program cannot join collinear objects.

The command OVERKILL will help to solve issues of collinear joining. To use the Overkill command, type the keyboard shortcut into the Command Line and press Enter. You will next need to specify the objects that you wish to overkill. Once you have selected all of the objects, you wish to overkill, press Enter and the Overkill dialog box (Image 5.2) will load. The default selections on the menu will solve most problems with joining objects, allowing you to click on the OK button. After completing the Overkill command, you should be able to join objects as long as they are touching.

Explode (X)

The command "Explode" is the exact opposite of the Join command and will explode objects into their most basic parts. This includes exploding objects such as rectangles and polylines into individual lines.

Offset (O)

The Offset command allows you to copy the geometry of an object and to offset it a defined distance from the original object. This allows you to create concentric circles, parallel lines and curves and to draw inset or outset closed polylines based on the geometry of a previously drawn object.

To use the Offset command, you must have an object drawn on the screen. Type the keyboard shortcut into the Command Line and press Enter or select the Ribbon button to begin the command. The Command Line will first ask you for the offset distance. To specify this distance, you can either type the distance into the Command Line or you can select two points on your drawing screen to define the distance.

Once the distance has been defined, the Command Line will prompt you to select the object you wish to offset. The program will offset only one object at a time. Once you have selected the object you wish to offset, you will be prompted to select a point on the side you wish to offset the item to. Move your cursor and click on the screen on the side to which you wish to draw the new geometry.

Once you have selected the side that you wish to offset the geometry to, the Offset command will automatically repeat beginning with prompting you to pick an item to offset. This command repeat will continue until you escape the command by pressing Enter or Escape.

The next time you enter the Offset command, the command will default to offset the same distance that you chose during the most recent use of this command. If you wish to use the previous offset distance, press Enter to accept the default or change the distance by typing the new dimension into the Command Line or selecting a distance on the screen before pressing enter.

All objects being offset during a single use of the Offset command will be offset to the same distance. If you wish to change the distance an

object is offset, you will need to exit and reenter the command to change the distance.

Fillet and Chamfer

As mentioned in Chapter 4, you can fillet and chamfer corners of a polyline using object modification tools. A fillet rounds over the corners of a polyline or adjacent lines (Image 5.3), while a chamfer will create an angle between those points (Image 5.4). AutoCAD allows you to specify dimensions for each of these modifications.

Fillet (F)

To use the Fillet command, enter the keyboard shortcut into the Command Line and press Enter or use the Ribbon button to enter the command.

The Fillet command defines the geometry based on the radius of the fillet. The command will always default to use the most recently defined radius. If you have not previously used the Fillet command during the drawing you are working in, the default for the fillet radius is 0, meaning there is no rounding of corners. To change the radius of the fillet being used, enter the command, and choose the Radius subcommand. The Command Line will prompt you to specify the fillet radius, which you can do by typing the dimension of the radius into the Command Line and pressing Enter.

Once the radius is defined, create the fillet by clicking on two adjacent lines with your cursor. Using the Polyline subcommand (P) will round over all corners of a polyline to the specified radius at one time. If you wish to fillet multiple objects using the same radius without having to exit and reenter the command for each object, you can use the Multiple subcommand.

Similar to the Trim and Extend commands, the Undo subcommand will allow you to undo a single fillet during the usage of the command. If you complete and escape the command, using the Undo command will undo all fillets created during the execution of the Fillet command.

Chamfer (CHA)

To begin the Chamfer command, type the keyboard shortcut into the Command Line and press Enter or select the button from the Modify panel on the Ribbon. The Chamfer button is located in a drop-down menu under the Fillet command. Click the arrow next to the Fillet command and then choose the Chamfer button. The Ribbon will change to add the most recently used button to the Modify panel, and put the other option in the drop-down window.

The Chamfer command defines the angle of the chamfer based on defined distances of the chamfer. Similar to the Fillet command, the Chamfer command defaults to using the most recently defined distances for chamfering. If you have not previously used this command in the drawing you are working in, the default will be o. To change the distance, use the Distance (D) subcommand. The Command Line will prompt you to enter the first chamfer distance, followed by the second chamfer distance. The first chamfer distance will be associated with the first line you choose on your chamfered objects, and the second distance will be associated with your second selection.

Alternately, you can define the angle of the chamfer by using the Angle subcommand instead of the Distance subcommand. If you choose to use the angle to define the chamfer, you will be prompted to enter the distance of the chamfer on the first edge, and then to enter the chamfer angle. Once again, the first chamfer distance will be associated with the first line you click on when selecting your chamfer location.

Similar to the Fillet command, once the chamfer distance or angle is set, you can create a chamfer by clicking on two adjacent lines with your cursor. Also, similar to the Fillet command, the Polyline subcommand within the Chamfer command will chamfer all corners of a polyline and the Multiple subcommand will allow you to chamfer several objects at once.

Using nonsymmetrical chamfers (different distances on either side of the angle) while chamfering a polyline can be a little strange. If you use the Polyline subcommand to do this, the chamfer will rotate counterclockwise around the polyline.

Chamfer and Fillet

It is possible to fillet corners of a previously chamfered polyline. You can select the newly drawn geometry of the chamfered corner when defining your fillet to round over chamfered corners. If you select the original two sides of the polyline, AutoCAD will erase the chamfered corner, and replace it with a fillet. If you hover your cursor over the drawing before selecting the geometry, a preview of the modification will appear on your screen so that you can see the result before defining the fillet.

Scale (SC)

The Scale command allows you to change the size of a previously drawn object by providing a factor to scale the object by. Enter the Scale command by clicking on the button in the Modify panel of the Ribbon or by entering the keyboard shortcut and pressing Enter. The Command Line will next ask you to select which objects you wish to scale and then to define a base point. The base point will remain in the same position on your screen and the scaled objects will grow or shrink from that point outward.

Finally, you will need to define the scale factor to use. A scale factor of one will keep the objects at their original size. Any scale factor greater than one will cause the objects to grow in size. A scale factor of two will cause the objects to double in size. A scale factor less than one will cause the objects to shrink in size. Using a scale factor of 48 on a drawing that was completed in quarter inch scale will scale that drawing to full size.

Before defining the scale factor, subcommands for Copy and Reference are available. The Copy subcommand will cause a copy of the objects to be created at the new scale factor and for the original objects to remain at their original size.

The Reference subcommand will allow you to select two points and then to define a new desired distance between those two points. At the completion of the Scale command, those two points will have the new desired distance between them and all objects selected as a part of the command will scale accordingly.

As the software in AutoCAD reads in units and not in dimensions, if you open a drawing that was created using Metric units and you are using Imperial units, the objects in the drawing will be much larger than they were originally drawn. As there are 25.4 millimeters in an inch, the drawing will be 25.4 times larger than it was drawn. The Scale command can be used to convert this to inches. To resize the Metric drawing to actual size in an Imperial drawing use a scale factor of 1/25.4. To change an Imperial drawing into Metric dimensions, you would use a scale factor of 25.4.

Align (AL)

The Align command allows you to move an object adjacent with another object by specifying source points on the object and specifying their destination points for where to move the object. The Align command is contained within the slide out at the bottom of the Modify panel on the Home tab of the Ribbon.

After entering the command, you will be asked to select an object or objects that you wish to align. Select only the objects that you wish to move and press Enter to indicate you have completed your selection. You will next be asked to select the first source point followed by the first destination point. Click a point on the object you wish to move as the source point and then click the point on the screen that you wish for that source point to be located at. Next you will need to click a second source point and destination point. Finally, you will have the option to choose a third source point and destination point.

If you choose three source and destination points, AutoCAD will move the object to the new location based on those three points. The first source point will be the control point and it will align with the destination point. The second and third points selected will define the rotation and alignment of the object being moved. They will be on the same plane as the destination points specified, but they may not actually touch their destination points.

If you select only two source and destination points, you will have the option to scale the object being moved based on the destination points so that the source points will touch their destination points.

Array (AR)

The Array command allows you to create several copies of a previously drawn object or set of objects. There are three types of two-dimensional arrays that all behave similarly. These are Rectangular Array, Polar Array and Array along a Path.

Rectangular Array

A rectangular array allows you to copy a previously drawn object into a series of rows and columns. To enter the Rectangular Array command, enter the keyboard shortcut into the Command Line and press Enter. Alternately, you can select the button from the Modify panel on the Ribbon. If you use the keyboard shortcut, you will be prompted to select the objects you wish to array, and then you will need to define the type of array you wish to perform. If you use the Ribbon panel button, you will only need to select the objects that you wish to array.

Once you have selected your objects, and selected the subcommand for the Rectangular Array in the Command Line, the Rectangular Array Creation tab will load in the Ribbon (Image 5.5). This tab holds the panels that allow you to create and manipulate a rectangular array. These panels allow you to set the numbers of columns and rows, and distance between each column and each row, and the total vertical and horizontal distance of the array.

When you have completed the array definition, press Enter, or choose the Close Array button on the Array Creation tab in the Ribbon. If you wish to change the definitions of the array, click on the array drawing within Model Space and the Array Creation tab will reload where you can redefine the array.

Polar Array

A polar array allows you to copy an object or set of objects around a defined center point. To enter the Polar Array command, enter the keyboard shortcut into the Command Line and press Enter or select the button from the Modify panel in the Ribbon. Note that the array commands are located in a slide-out menu on the Modify panel. The most recently used array command is set to the home position with the other array commands located in the slide-out menu.

Once you have entered the Array command, select the object(s) you wish to array and then select the Polar Array subcommand. Next you will need to define the center point of the array.

Once you have selected the center point of the array, the Polar Array Creation tab will load in the Ribbon (Image 5.6). Within this Ribbon tab, panels allow you to specify the number of items within the array, the rotation angle between each item and the rotation angle that the array fills. You can also choose to rotate the array around the base point, or to change the direction of the array about the circle. Increasing the rows of the array in the Ribbon creates spokes of the arrayed objects about the center point of the array extending out from the center point. Changing the levels is a three-dimensional command that increases the arrays stacked on top of each other in the Z axis.

Path Array

Arraying objects along a path works in much the same way as both of the array commands above. The Path Array command requires a defined path such as an arc, polyline or spline to array itself along. The path must be drawn within the AutoCAD drawing window prior to the array creation as the selection of the path is needed to define the array.

Enter the Array command in the same method as above, select the object(s) you wish to array, and then select the Path Array subcommand. Finally, you will need to choose the path that you will use to define the array. This can be a line, a polyline, an arc or a spline.

Once you have defined the path, the object(s) will array themselves along the path and the Path Array Creation tab will load in the Ribbon (Image 5.7).

Within the Path Array Creation tab, Ribbon panels allow you to select the number of items within the array and the distance between each object. Changing the rows is similar to changing the rows in the polar array as this creates more spokes around a curve or rows along a path. Once again, changing the levels of the array is a three-dimensional command that draws arrays on top of one another in the Z axis.

6

LAYER AND PROPERTY MANAGERS

In the previous two chapters, we have covered tools that allow you to create and modify geometric objects. In this chapter, we will discuss ways to assign properties to these objects that allow you to better organize larger drawings, define materials, line types and line weights, and to cycle through objects within the drawing screen.

Layers

The use of layers is the primary method for organizing objects within an AutoCAD drawing. Objects can be placed on individual layers based on function, purpose, material choice or other factors. The use of layers can reduce the visual complexity of a drawing by allowing you to turn off or "freeze" groups of objects that you do not need to see or modify at a particular moment.

Tool Palettes

Tool palettes hold a specific set of tools within each palette. The most commonly used tool palette is the Ribbon; however, there are many other tool palettes and toolbars available within AutoCAD. Tool palettes can be minimized and docked to the side of your drawing window, or can be extended to a second monitor.

Within a tool palette called the Layer Property Manager (Image 6.1) AutoCAD allows you to create custom layers with custom layer names for each drawing you are working with. Within the layer creation, you can define the line weight, line type, print functionality and the color of the objects drawn on that particular layer as well as the transparency of three-dimensional objects drawn on a particular layer. The Layer Property Manager can be accessed by clicking the Layer Properties button on the Layer Panel of the Home tab of the Ribbon or by typing the command LAYER into the Command Line and pressing Enter. Once the palette is on the screen, you can dock it to one side of the screen by clicking and holding the side bar of the palette and hovering over the extreme edge of the drawing area, or drag it to a secondary monitor. You can also minimize the palette by toggling through the minimize arrows at the top right of the palette. If the palette has been minimized, hovering the cursor over the palette will open the palette and allow you to access the functions within.

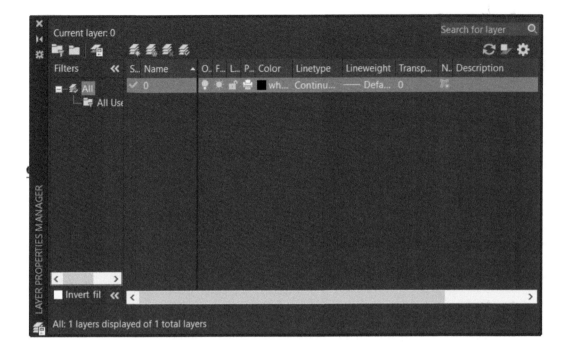

While the Layer Property Manager allows you to create new layers, the Layer Panel on the Ribbon allows you to assign objects to layers and to manipulate the ways in which objects assigned to these layers behave.

Creating New Layers

When you first open a clean AutoCAD drawing, there are two default layers loaded into the drawing, Layer 0 and Defpoints. Layer 0 is the default printing layer, while Defpoints is the default non-printing layer. It is good drafting practice to create new layers prior to beginning drafting and to draw objects on the user created layers. Layers can be saved in drawing templates, preventing the need to create new layers every time you begin a new drafting.

Layer Names

With the Layer Property Manager on the screen and opened, right-click within the window to load a list of available actions. Buttons above the "Name" column in the Layer Property Manager replicate the major functions available in the right-click menu. These actions include the ability to rename or delete a layer. To create a new layer, click on "New Layer." The first new layer created will default to a layer name of Layer 1. The name Layer 1 will be highlighted, allowing you to type over the text with a new layer name. Certain symbols are not allowed within layer names. Once you have appropriately named the layer, press Enter. You can rename layers after their creation by right-clicking on the layer within the Layer Property Manager and selecting the "Rename layer" option from the right-click menu.

Layer Color

Changing the color setting so that objects on different layers appear as different colors on your drawing window is one of the easiest ways to organize a larger drawing and to differentiate between objects. When you create a new layer, clicking on the small white box under the Layer Color heading will take you to the Color Selection window. Here, you can choose between standard index colors, a true color scroll bar, and change color books to different hues to allow you to select what color the objects on that layer will appear on your drawing window.

While plot styles are discussed later in this text, it is helpful to know that layer color will have an effect on how objects are printed if you are using a color dependent plot table, which will cause all objects of the same color to be plotted identically. Index colors must be used when using color dependent plot tables.

Line Type

The Line Type selection in the Layer Property Manger allows you to define the type of line that will appear on a printed page for each object drawn on this layer.

When creating a new layer, all line types are set to the default of a continuous line. To change the line type, left-click on the line type (the word continuous), which will take you to the Line Type selection menu (Image 6.2). The Line Type selection menu will have a list of all line types currently loaded into the drawing. When beginning a clean AutoCAD drawing, only the Continuous line type is loaded. To load other line types, click the "Load" button at the bottom of the menu.

Select the line types that you wish to load into this particular drawing. Hold CTRL to select multiple line types, or shift to choose all line types between two selections. Once all of the line types you wish to use are selected press "OK."

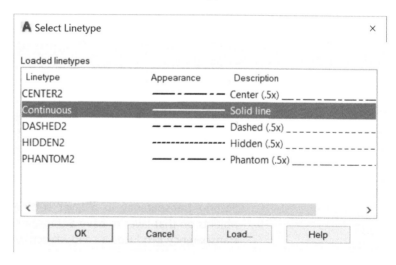

This will take you back to the Line Type selection menu where you can select the line type for the current layer.

Often, within a certain line type, there are several options for that particular line type that have to do with the length of the individual parts of a broken line. For example, options within the line type selection menu include Center, Center (.5x) and Center (2X). The Center (2x) draws the individual parts of the broken center line twice as big as the standard center line, while the Center (.5x) draws those half as long and twice as often.

Line types can be loaded and saved into template drawings to prevent needing to reload line types for individual drafting files. For theatrical drafting, it is recommended that you have Hidden, Dashed, Center and Phantom line types along with Continuous loaded into your template files.

Line Weights

The Line Weight setting allows you to define the printed thickness of lines of all objects on a defined layer. When creating a new layer, all line weights are set to a default line weight entitled "Default." The initial value for the default line weight is 0.01 inches or 0.25 mm.

AutoCAD also defaults all line weights to metric dimensions until changed by the user. To change these settings, you will need to access the Line Weight Settings menu (Image 6.3) by typing "LW" into the Command Line and pressing Enter. Within this menu, you can toggle between inches and millimeters to define line weights, define the thickness of the default line weight and choose whether or not to view line weights on your drawing screen. The viewing of line weights in model space can be toggled on and off using the Line Weight Display button included on the Function Bar. Turning off the option to display line weights in your drawing window will help save processor space and speed up your drafting process. While printed line weights are controlled by settings within plot style tables, those tables default to printing the line weights as defined by their layer properties.

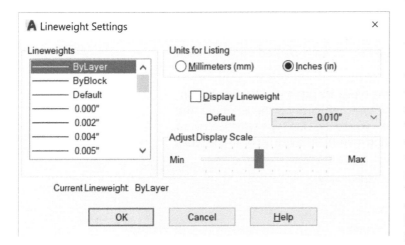

Transparency

Setting transparency in a layer setting sets all three-dimensional objects on that layer to have a transparent view when printed. A 0% transparency produces a solid object, while increasing the transparency creates translucent and transparent three-dimensional objects. To save processor speed while drafting, you can toggle the Show/Hide Transparency button on the Function Bar at the bottom of your screen so that objects will print as translucent or transparent, but won't show as such within your drawing window.

Plot Layers

There may be times that you have drawn objects (such as construction lines) in your drawing window that you may not wish to plot to the printed page. Within the Layer Property Manager, clicking on the icon of the printer under the Plot column will toggle the option to not print any objects drawn on that particular layer. The Defpoints layer can also be used as a non-printing layer, and cannot be turned into a printing layer.

Turning Off vs. Freezing Layers

In the Layer Property Manager, just to the right of the layer name are two icons that allow you to control the visibility of layers. These icons are duplicated in the Layer panel on the Ribbon and serve the same function in both locations.

The icon of the light bulb allows you to "Turn off" a layer. Turning a layer off hides all objects drawn on that layer from the user. It helps to clean the screen and hide objects you are not currently working with. Clicking the light bulb again turns the layer back on. You can also use the commands LAYOFF and LAYON to turn layers off and on, respectively.

The icon of the sun allows you to "Freeze" a layer. (The icon turns to a snow flake when the layer is frozen.) Freezing a layer not only hides the objects drawn on that layer from the user, it also removes that information from the system memory. When an object is frozen, AutoCAD will treat the object as though it does not exist. For example, using Erase/All to clean your screen will erase objects on layers that are turned off, but will not erase objects on frozen layers. Clicking the snowflake thaws the layer turning it back on. You can also use the commands LAYF and THAW to freeze and thaw layers.

In the Layer panel of the Ribbon are two more buttons that allow you to turn on all layers and thaw all layers.

Locking a Layer

The icon of the padlock allows you to lock a layer in its current state. Locking a layer will prevent you from making changes to any object drawn on that particular layer, or from drawing new items or deleting items from that layer. The icon is duplicated in the Layer panel on the Ribbon and serves the same function in both locations.

Working with Layers

Once layers have been created, those layers are manipulated using the  tools on the Layer panel of the Ribbon. Many of the functions, such as freezing layers, that are available within the Layer Property Manager are duplicated here. The ability to set objects to layers and to select the layer on which to draw new objects are housed within the Layer Control Bar (Image 6.4) located on the Layer panel of the Ribbon.

Drawing Objects on Layers and Moving Objects between Layers

To draw a new object on a defined layer, click on the arrow next to the Layer Control Bar on the Ribbon, scroll down to select the layer you wish to draw new objects on and left-click to select that layer. All new objects will be drawn on the selected layer until you do this again to change to another layer. The current layer and its properties will remain in this bar for reference. A layer that is either turned off, frozen or locked cannot be made the current layer as no new objects will appear on layers in these states.

To change a previously drawn object to a new layer, first select the object(s) that you wish to move to the new layer. Once the objects are selected, click on the arrow next to the Layer Control Bar in the Ribbon, scroll down and select the layer that you wish to move these objects to by left-clicking on the selected layer. All selected objects will move to the layer selected. If the selected layer is turned off or frozen, the objects will become invisible. If the layer you have selected has been locked, you will be unable to move these objects to that layer until you have first unlocked the layer.

Make Objects Layer Current

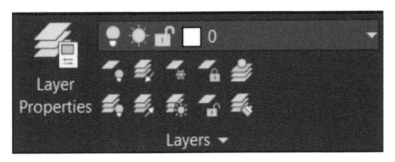

The button "Make Object's Layer Current" located in the Layer panel of the Ribbon (Image 6.5) allows you to change layers to the layer of a previously drawn object. Click on the Ribbon tool, then click on an object that is drawn on the layer you wish to switch to. All newly drawn objects will now be drawn on the same layer as the object you selected.

Match Layer Properties (MA)

This command allows you to change objects from their current layer to the layer of another object drawn on the screen. Enter the command through the use of the keyboard shortcut or the Ribbon button, select an object with the destination layer you wish to use, and then select all objects you wish to transfer to this layer. Press ESC to finish the command and discontinue moving objects to the new layer.

Previous

The "Previous" button undoes the most recent changes you made to layers without the need to undo other commands, such as the drawing of new objects. This command is located on the Ribbon slide-out menu, which is accessed by clicking on the arrow at the bottom of the Layer panel on the Ribbon.

Layer Isolate (LAYISO) and Unisolate

These buttons allow you to hide all objects drawn on the screen other than those objects drawn on a selected group of layers. Enter the Layer Isolate command, either through the keyboard shortcut or the use of the Ribbon button, select all layers you wish to continue to see, and then press Enter. All layers other than those selected will be turned off, hiding them from your view. The Unisolate Layers button will turn all layers back on.

Isolate Objects (ISOLATE)

If you wish to isolate single objects, instead of all objects on an entire layer, the Isolate command will isolate a select group of objects, without reference to layers. Enter the command, select all objects you wish to isolate and then press Enter. All other objects will be hidden from the screen. Alternatively, you can select the objects that you wish to isolate first and then load the right-click shortcut menu where you will have access to the Isolate tools. The Unisolate (UNISO) command will turn all objects back on.

To hide an object or selection of objects, use the command Hide Objects (HIDEOB). This command is the exact opposite of the Isolate command and functions in the same way.

Miscellaneous Layer Options

In the slide out at the bottom of the Layer panel on the Ribbon are several other commands that allow you to further manipulate how layers work, and what objects are drawn on which layers. These include the ability to copy objects and have the copy of the original placed on a new layer, the ability to merge two layers into one and to delete layers and all objects drawn on that layer and the ability to do a layer walk. Performing a layer walk will isolate each layer successively, showing you each layer and the objects drawn thereon.

Object Properties

Similar to the Layer Properties Manager, the Properties Manager has both a tool palette and a panel on the Ribbon that perform different functions. To open the Properties Manager tool palette, use the keyboard shortcut CH, click on the diagonal arrow at the bottom right of the Properties panel on the Ribbon or navigate through the Menu Bar by selecting Tools/Palettes/Properties. You may also access the Properties menu by first selecting an object, loading the right-click Shortcut menu and selecting "Properties" at the bottom of the menu.

When no object is selected, the Properties Manager (Image 6.6) will provide you with general information about the drawing you are currently working in, including the current layer, line type and line weight of newly drawn objects, as well as the current distance from the X, Y, Z origin point that your cursor is on the screen.

When an object is selected, the Properties Manager will provide you with information about that object including the layer, color and line type of the object. The Properties Manager will also give you the length of lines, dimensions of

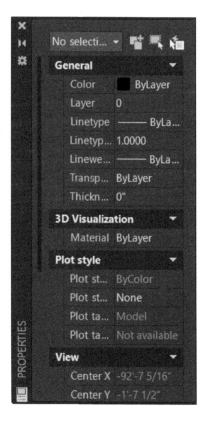

closed polylines such as rectangles, including area, information about and the ability to override dimensions, the ability to set plot styles for different pages, etc. The properties displayed in the Properties Manager will change depending on the objects currently selected.

The Properties Manager will provide you with information about objects selected on the screen, while the Properties panel on the Ribbon will let you manipulate the properties of objects drawn on the screen. Within the Properties panel of the Ribbon you can select the color of objects, their line weight and line type. Selecting "By Layer" in each of these settings is the default, and AutoCAD will revert to the layer settings for this information. However, selecting anything other than "By Layer" will override the layer settings and the objects selected will be displayed as defined within the object properties.

7

BLOCKS AND BLOCK EDITING

To this point in the text, we have discussed drawing individual shapes as a means for drafting scenic elements. As lumber and building materials are shapes by definition, knowing how to use the program to draw shapes gives us the tools necessary to create drawings of scenic elements that are easily editable. Other tools, like the Layer Property Manager, allow us to organize drawings so that they are easier to work with.

There are many times when we use the same scenic elements throughout a set, or even more frequently when the same style of lighting instrument is included several times in a light plot. While the ability to copy and paste these elements around the drawing saves the process of drawing, these anew in each circumstance, if these objects need editing once they have been drawn and placed, it would be time consuming to have to edit each instance of an object, or to have to redo the copy and paste process after editing a single instance.

AutoCAD allows the user to gather a group of objects together into an association called a block. These can be single objects as simple as a single line, or a large group of objects that are associated together. Almost anything can be combined into a single block, and it is up to the user to find the best way to use blocks to complete the drafting project they are working with.

A block is meant to be a repeatable instance of a group of objects. Once defined, blocks can be edited, and editing the geometry of one instance of the block will also edit all other instances of blocks with the same name within the drawing file. In a theatrical scenic drawing, using a block for a stock platform is a common use, as all stock platforms of that size would have the same geometry.

If a block is only being used once within a drawing, it will actually take more processing space than the individual components of the block. However, blocks can save processing space within the program if they are being used multiple times within the drawing. The first occurrence of the block holds the memory for all geometry contained within the block, as well as the information for the block name and the block insertion. Every additional occurrence of the block only holds the information for the block insertion, adding only one additional entity of memory for each block insertion.

Blocks previously created within the drawing file can be entered into the drawing, whether there is a current instance of the block in the drawing window or not, and block libraries can be created that allow users to pull previously created blocks into their drawings. Many of these block libraries, including several libraries of lighting instruments, are freely available online and can be downloaded for use in individual drawings.

Creating Blocks

There are two methods for creating blocks. The most common workflow is to create the geometry of the block first and then to combine that geometry into a block definition. The second method is to create a block definition first and then to create the geometry.

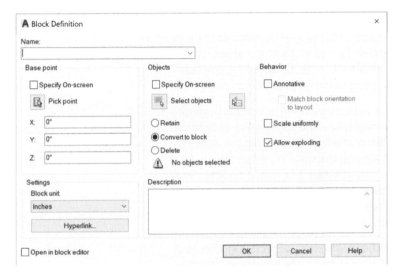

To create a block using the first method, begin by drawing the geometry for the first instance of the block in Model Space. Once the geometry is completed, enter the command BLOCK (B) into the Command Line and press Enter or navigate to the Insert tab of the Ribbon and choose Create Block from the Block Definition panel. This will load the Block Definition dialog box. (Image 7.1)

To create a block definition prior to creating the geometry for a block, enter the command "BE" into the Command Line and press Enter to load the Edit Block Definition window. Type the name for the new block and click "OK." The Block Editor will open where you can begin creating geometry for the block.

Naming Blocks

New blocks must use unique names. If you use a name for an already existing block, the new block geometry will overwrite the existing block. If you enter a block name for the new block that is being used for another block, AutoCAD will ask you to confirm that you wish to overwrite the existing block.

Base Points and Object Selection

When creating blocks, you will need to select the base point of the block. When inserting a new copy of this block, the base point will act as the insertion point for this block. If you have created the geometry of the block first, you will also need to select the objects to be included in the block. It is usually easiest to check both of these boxes to "select on screen," which will allow you to point and click with your cursor to select the insertion point and to use selection windows to select which objects should be included in your new block.

Object Selection

Within the Objects panel of the Block Definition palette, there are three buttons to choose from that determine the behavior of the objects selected once the block is created. Selecting the "Retain" option will create a block with the object definition selected, but will retain the original objects without turning them into blocks. Selecting "Convert to Block" will create the block definition, and convert the objects selected into an instance of the new block, with those objects remaining in their current on-screen position. Selecting "Delete" will create a block definition of the objects while deleting the original objects from the drawing window.

Exploding Blocks

When creating blocks in the Block Definition dialog box, there is an option to "Allow Exploding." Having this box checked will allow you to explode blocks with this block definition within the drawing file. Exploding a block removes the block definition from a specific instance of the block while keeping the geometry of the block. Essentially, this allows the user to tell the program that you no longer wish for this particular set of geometry to be associated with that block definition, allowing you to make edits to the geometry without changing the definition of the block.

Block Unit Settings

When you create a block, you also need to set the block units. It is important that the units for your block match your drawing units within the drawing file. This will ensure that blocks are inserted at the correct size and that there are no scaling issues due to the use of separate unit definitions.

Inserting Blocks

Once a block definition is created within a drawing, it will exist until it is purged from the drawing by the user. (Purging will be discussed later in this chapter.) Even if there is not an instance of the block drawn within the file, the definition will still exist within the drawing file. This allows for insertion of previously defined blocks.

To insert a block into your drawing, navigate to the Insert tab on the Ribbon and click on the "Insert" button in the Block panel. If you wish to insert a block from an existing block library, click on "Blocks from Libraries." A File Manager window will open allowing you to define the file location of the block you wish to use. The most recently used blocks in the current drawing will appear as a small image along with their block name when you click on the Insert button. To choose one of these blocks, click on the block you wish to insert and define the insert location by clicking on the screen.

Clicking on "Recent Blocks" will load the Block Manager (Image 7.2). As with the Layer Property Manager and Properties Manager, the Block Manager can be moved and docked to the side of the screen or moved to a secondary monitor.

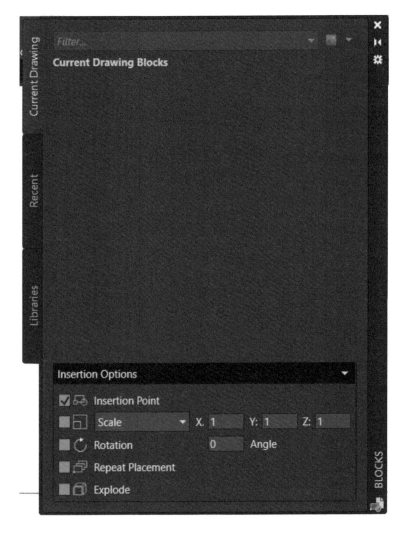

The Block Manager provides access to block definitions that exist within the current drawing as well as blocks that you have recently used in other drawings and any blocks you have saved to block libraries.

Once you have selected which block to insert, you will need to define the insertion point by clicking on the screen. You will also need to specify the scale of the block (almost always a 1:1 scale) as well as specifying a rotation angle for the block. Blocks can be scaled and rotated after they are inserted into the drawing, so it is usually okay to leave these at their defaults and work within the drawing window of Model Space once the block has been inserted.

Editing Block Geometry

There are two ways to edit the geometry of blocks within AutoCAD. The first one is to use the Refedit tool bar. This method allows you the use of almost all of the drawing tools within AutoCAD and allows you to view the block in the drawing window as well as how it may interact with other nearby geometry.

The second way to edit blocks is to open the block in the Block Editor. Opening a block in a Block Editor allows you more tools to define the block and to manipulate how the block acts, but only allows you to view the block itself without viewing other objects drawn in the drawing window.

Refedit Toolbar

To access the Refedit toolbar, select the Tools panel from the Menu Bar, select Toolbars, AutoCAD and scroll down to REFEDIT at the bottom of the list of toolbars. Once this is checked, the Refedit toolbar will appear on your screen (Image 7.3). Alternatively, you can type "REFEDIT" into the Command Line and press Enter to load the Refedit toolbar. This toolbar can be docked or extended to a second screen, similar to other toolbars and palettes within the program.

Clicking the button to the far left of this toolbar will allow you to choose a block to edit. Once you

click this button, select the block you wish to work with by clicking on the block and pressing Enter. Once you have entered the "Edit reference in place" function, any new geometry created will be included in all definitions of the block, as will any other changes made. You can also use the "Add to working set" button to add previously created objects to the block definition, or the "Remove from working set" button to remove geometry from the block definition. When you are finished with changes you wish to make to the block, you can use the buttons on the toolbar to either save the block definition with the changes, or to discard the changes made to the block.

All drawing tools available within AutoCAD are available when editing a block, with the exception of the Block and Array tools. Block definitions can have other blocks included in them, but when you are editing a block, you are unable to create a new block. As the Array command creates a block of objects in a specific formation, the Array commands are also unavailable during a block editing session.

Block Editor

The second option for editing blocks is to use the Block Editor. The Block Editor is a drawing space that allows you to create and modify a specific block definition. The Block Editor is organized to prioritize tools for working with blocks (Image 7.4). Within the

Block Editor, many more functions for defining and controlling the behavior of a block are available. All of the functions available within the Refedit toolbar are available here, as well as the ability to include attribute definitions that can be changed per instance of the block, and the ability to create dynamic blocks that have rules about visibility and behavior based on user commands. Attribute definitions and dynamic blocks will be covered in the following chapters.

Mirroring Blocks

It is important to be careful when using the Mirror command in conjunction with the use of blocks. Mirror parts are not always the same part. When a block is mirrored, it will appear correct when viewed on the computer screen; however, if the original block is used to create machine and manufactured parts, it is possible to create original parts when you should be creating mirror parts.

Nested Copy (NCOPY)

Using the Copy command with a block reference will cause the entire block to be copied and pasted around the screen. If you wish to copy a single object from within a block, you can use the Nested Copy command. This command will allow you to select a single piece of geometry from within a block and have a copy of it pasted to your drawing window. Using the Multiple subcommand will allow you to paste multiple copies of the geometry. The new objects will not be associated with the block definition.

Nested Block

It is possible, and sometimes desired, to nest blocks inside of other blocks. This process allows one or multiple block definitions to exist within a larger block definition. I often use this method in drafting stage decking. In this process, individual platforms exist as block definitions. An area of the stage deck then also exists as a block definition that includes the individual platform units.

Purge (PU)

The Purge command loads a dialog box (Image 7.5) that allows you to remove unused items from your AutoCAD file. Items that can be purged from drawings include but are not limited to block definitions, unused layers and line types, plot styles and text styles. You may either select specific items to be purged from a drawing or use the "Purge All" button to remove all unused items from the drawing file. Purging unused items can be a helpful tool to manage file sizes.

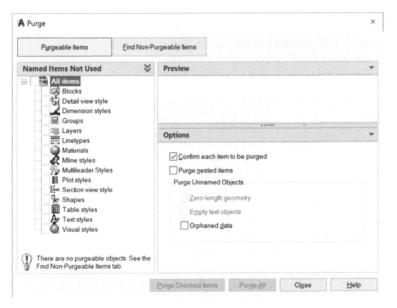

If you copy an instance of a block into a file, where a block by the same name already exists, the block being copied will be overwritten to match the geometry of the existing block definition. If you wish to keep the geometry of the block being copied into the drawing, you would first need to purge the existing block definition from the file.

8

CREATING TITLE BLOCKS AND REFERENCE LINES

In this chapter, we will discuss how to use the Block Editor to create title blocks and reference lines in an AutoCAD file, and how to use attribute definitions within the Block Editor to allow the user to change information within them. Once these items have been created, they can be saved to a template file, eliminating the need to create them each time you begin drafting.

Text

To this point in the book, we have covered how to create geometry within the program. Before we begin discussing creating title blocks and reference lines, it is helpful to discuss how to enter text into AutoCAD.

There are two types of text that AutoCAD will recognize. Text (DT or TEXT) will provide a single line of text without the ability to return to start a new line of text, while Multiline text (MTEXT) will return to a new line of text when you press the Return/Enter key on your keyboard.

Text Styles

The Annotate tab of the Ribbon holds information about the current text style being used. AutoCAD comes preinstalled with a standard text style. This text style can be modified and new text styles can be added using the Text Style dialog box (Image 8.1). To access this dialog box, navigate to the Annotate tab of the Ribbon and click on the diagonal arrow at the bottom right corner of the Text Panel. You can also access the Text Style dialog box by using the keyboard entry STYLE.

From the Text Style dialog box you can modify existing text styles or create new ones. To create a new text style, click on the

"New" button to the right of the box, name the new text style in the pop-up window and click "OK." With the name of the new text style highlighted, use the selections to define font name and font style. Text height is measured in the printed height of the text on the page. Text styles can be saved in drawing template files, preventing the need create them each time you begin drafting.

Standard vs. Annotative Text

AutoCAD added Layout tabs to their software in the year 2000 (discussed in Chapter 9). Prior to this, all notation and dimensioning was completed in the Model Space tab. The industry standard now is to insert text and dimensions in the Layout tab. This allows you to use "Standard" text where you will define the text height as it will appear on the printed page.

Annotative text allows you to enter text into Model Space, and to define what scale your drawing will be printed at to set the text to the correct size for printing. As the industry standard is to enter text and dimensions within layout tabs, this book will assume that method.

Entering Text

To enter a text box, select the style of text you wish to use (Text or Multiline text) by pressing the appropriate button on the Ribbon or entering the command in the Command Line and pressing Enter. Select the start point for the text box, and then select the opposite corner for the text box. When you have defined a Multiline text box area, the Ribbon will load the Text Editor (Image 8.2). The Text Editor functions in much the same manner as a word processor, allowing you to change

the properties of the text, justify text, insert bullets and numbering, change line spacing, create columns, insert symbols and even spell check your work.

Use your keyboard to enter the desired text into the text box. To escape either text command, use the Escape key on your keyboard.

If you wish to extend or shrink the size of a text box, click on the text and use the grips to adjust the size of the text box. You can also use the Move and Rotate commands to adjust the position and direction of text after it has been inserted into your drawing.

Creating Title Blocks

Title blocks are created in a similar fashion used in Chapter 7 to create blocks of geometry. You can either begin by opening the Block Editor (BE) and creating the title block within that window or you can create geometry and text in the model window and then convert it to a block. Text commands are used to create static text (any text that remains the same in every instance of the block). Any text that will change within the title block (such as a plate number) will be added as an attribute definition.

Sketching out a title block on a piece of scratch paper will assist you in creating a title block in AutoCAD. When you have completed your title block, it can be saved to your template drawing for use in future AutoCAD files.

Begin with drafting the geometry of your title block, including the page border. Once your geometry is drawn, use the Text commands to enter static text in your title block. Ensure that your page border is drawn to a size within the printable area of a page. While an Arch D sheet is $24'' \times 36''$ no plotter will print to the edge of this paper, which means that if you draw your page border at $24'' \times 36''$ it will not be printed.

Attribute Definitions

Information entered into a block as text will remain the same in each occurrence of the block. This follows the same principles of the way geometry behaves within block definitions. Many times there is a need for information to change from one occurrence of a title block to the next. This may include the name of the show the drafting is for, the name of the theatre, etc. and will certainly include the plate numbers of each drafting plate. To accommodate this need for changes within a block definition, attribute definitions can be used.

An attribute is a tag or label that associates specific information with specific instances of a block. This information is located in the same location on every instance of the block; however, this information is included as a variable, allowing the attribute definition to change between block occurrences. In more complicated drawings, attribute definitions can be extracted from block references to create a spreadsheet or database of parts to be purchased. Multiple attributes can be assigned to a block, provided that they all have different tags or attribute names.

Attribute definitions are created using the Attribute Definition dialog box (Image 8.3). If you are creating your title block in the Block Editor, navigate to the Block Editor tab of the Ribbon and click "Attribute Definition" in the Action Parameters Panel. If you are creating your title block in model space, navigate to the Insert tab of the Ribbon and click on "Define Attributes" in the Block Definition panel. You can also use the keyboard command ATT to load the Attribute Definition dialog box from either location.

Attribute

On the right side of the Attribute Definition dialog box is a section titled "Attribute." Here you will need to specify a tag and a prompt. You are also given the option to enter a default value, although entering the default value is not required.

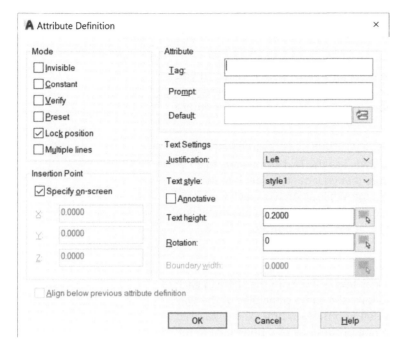

The tag is a name you assign for this attribute definition. This name will need to be unique and not repeated as an attribute definition within the drawing file. The tag name cannot contain spaces. The prompt is the question you will be asked when you insert this block to define this attribute. For example, a prompt may be given as "Show Name" at which time you would input the name of the production the drafting packet is for.

The default value is a value that will automatically fill in for individual tags. If the prompt "Show Name" were to appear in the Command Line, and the default value was "Show A," pressing the Enter button without typing anything would cause "Show A" to be the definition for the attribute in this occurrence of the block.

Clicking on the "Insert Field" button to the right of the Default text area will load a field category box. This "Field" toolbox will load information from the drawing save file to be the default text in your Attribute Definition. For example, choosing the Date Field as a default for a prompt will cause the date of the most recent save of the drawing file to be the default text for this attribute definition.

Modes

On the left of the dialog box are selection boxes to specify attribute modes. Modes control the behavior of the attribute as it is inserted into the drawing file.

Selecting Invisible will cause the attribute not to appear on the screen. The attribute will hold data, which can be extracted, but that data will be invisible to the user.

Selecting Constant will cause the attribute to provide the same data, not allowing you to change that data in separate instances of the attribute.

Selecting Verify will cause AutoCAD to ask you to verify attribute definitions when they are entered. AutoCAD will ask you for the attribute definition when the title block is inserted. After you have input the information, AutoCAD will again ask you to reenter that information to verify it. Both definitions will need to be identical for AutoCAD to accept them.

Selecting Preset will cause AutoCAD to input the default value for attributes when the title block is inserted into the drawing.

Lock Position locks the position of the attribute within the title block once it is placed, not allowing you to move the attribute unless you uncheck the block first.

Multiple Lines will cause the attribute definition to act as a Multiline text instead of a single line text.

Text Settings

On the right of the Attribute Definition dialog box, you will need to select the text settings for this attribute. Text styles saved into the drawing will be loaded into dialog box and are available to be selected. You also will specify the text justification (left, center, right, etc.).

Insertion Point

You have three options for specifying the insertion point of an attribute. The first is to specify the insertion point on screen. Checking this box will allow you to click on the screen with your mouse to define the insertion point after clicking "OK" to finalize the attribute definition. Unchecking "Specify on Screen" will allow you to enter the X, Y, Z coordinates for the insertion point on screen.

Beginning with the second attribute definition you create, you will also have the ability to choose "Align below Previous Attribute Definition." Choosing this option will ensure that text in attribute definitions are aligned with one another.

Saving Blocks

Once you have the geometry, text and attributes for your title block, you will need to save it as a block definition. If you created your title block in model space, this follows the same pattern as creating blocks of geometry as discussed in Chapter 7, using the Block Definition (B) dialog box.

If you created your title block in the Block Editor, there is a button on the left-hand side of the Ribbon in the Block Editor tab to save your block. You are unable to save drawing files when you are in the Block Editor, but this button will save your work within the block. To close the Block Editor, click on "Close Block Editor" on the right side of the Block Editor tab in the Ribbon. If you have made changes to the block definition since it was last saved, a window will appear prompting you to either save the changes and close the block, discard the changes and close the block or to cancel and re-enter the Block Editor.

Testing Blocks

At any point during a block editing session, you can test the function of the attribute definitions using the Test Block command. To enter this command, use the "Test Block" panel button on the left-hand side of the Ribbon in the Block Editor. This will open a new AutoCAD window that allows you to test the block functionality. The Test Block window will allow the block to function as though it had been inserted into a new file and allow you to input the information for the attribute definitions and to view the finished title block. When you are finished, choosing the "Close Test Block" on the right side of the window will return you to the Block Editor where you can continue to make revisions to the block.

Creating Reference Lines

The process for creating reference lines is almost identical to the process for creating a title block. Create the geometry and the text for the reference line, using attribute definitions for any text that may change in separate instances of the block. When creating the attribute for the notes within the reference line, selecting the Multiple Lines mode will allow the text to function as a Multiline text instead of a single line text.

Inserting and Editing Blocks

Upon insertion of a block with attribute definitions, the Edit Attributes dialog box (Image 8.4) will load, allowing you to define the attributes for this instance of the block. If you chose default text for an attribute, it will appear in the attribute definition. Once the attributes are edited as desired, click OK on the bottom of the window to exit the window and the block will populate with attributes as defined.

Enhanced Attribute Editor

Once an attributed block has been inserted into a drawing, you can open the Enhanced Attribute Editor (Image 8.5) by double clicking anywhere on the block. Within the Enhanced Attribute Editor, you can redefine the attributes for this instance of the block, as well as changing the size and style of text for the attribute in this block occurrence, and changing the layer, color and properties of the attribute for this block occurrence.

Block Attribute Manager

Block Attributes can be edited using the Block Attribute Manager (BATT-MAN) dialog box (Image 8.6). With the dialog box loaded, select the block you wish to edit, either by using the button on the left to select the block on screen or by using the menu on the right to navigate to and select the block you wish to edit.

Choose the attribute you wish to edit by clicking on it so that it is highlighted within the list on the left. Moving attributes up and down will cause them to switch places both within the list and within the block. The Edit button will load the Edit Attribute dialog box. The remove button will remove the attribute from the block definition. Clicking the Settings button at the bottom will load a dialog box that allows you to view and change the settings of individual attributes.

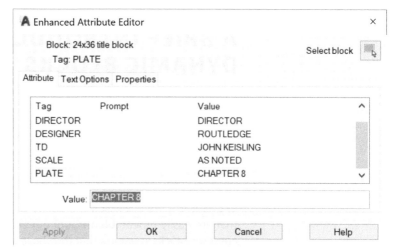

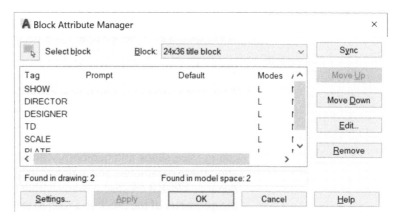

9

A BRIEF INTRODUCTION TO DYNAMIC BLOCKS

In Chapter 7, we discussed the ability to use blocks to create objects that are easily repeatable throughout an individual file. Those blocks are static blocks, meaning that they have a single state of existence and will appear identical in each block occurrence. In this chapter, we will discuss the ability to create blocks with geometry that can have more than one state of existence and is alterable in each block occurrence. These blocks are referred to as dynamic blocks.

What Is a Dynamic Block?

A block is a group of objects that can be copied throughout the drawing, allowing editing in one block to change the geometry of all other blocks with the same name. There is also an option to create rules, called parameters and actions that allow you to insert a block that can change size, shape and geometry within the block. The process for creating these parameters and actions can be time consuming, but once a dynamic block is created, a menu within the block allows you to select the geometry of the block you wish to exist within each block instance, significantly reducing drafting time.

The option to create dynamic blocks is not available within AutoCAD for Mac; however, dynamic blocks that were previously created with a Windows platform can be used and manipulated within AutoCAD for Mac.

Constraints

Constraints create a set of rules about how geometry behaves in relation to other geometry. There are two types of constraints that can be used, Geometric constraints and Dimensional constraints. Geometric constraints define how objects align to one another while Dimensional constraints control the size of geometry within an object or drawing. Constraints can be added to geometry within Model Space using the Parametric tab of the Ribbon (Image 9.1) or can be added to geometry

within the Block Editor using the tools located within the Geometric and Dimensional panels of the Block Editor Ribbon. Constraints can be applied to any geometry whether or not it is included in a block definition. Constraints included in a block definition can be edited in each occurrence of the block without affecting the geometry in other block occurrences.

Constraints are applied to geometry by first selecting the constraint you wish to use and then clicking on the geometry you wish to constrain in the drawing window. When applying constraints, the first item of geometry that you select will act as the default geometry, meaning that if you apply an Equal constraint to two lines, select the first line as the line you wish to use for the length. The second line you select will change in size to become equal in length to the first line selected. Changing the length of the first line after applying the constraint will also change the length of the second line so that the two remain equal in length.

Geometric constraints can be used to make geometry coincidental, collinear, tangential to a circle or arc, parallel, perpendicular or concentric. Geometry can also be constrained so that it is always horizontal or vertical, or affixed to a point. Multiple constraints can, and often are, applied to an object. When a constraint has been applied to geometry, a Constraint Bar will appear next to the geometry in the drawing window. Hovering over this Constraint Bar will highlight the constraint for that geometry as well as the geometry it is constrained to. The Show/Hide button in the Ribbon will hide these Constraint Bars. If a Constraint Bar is hidden, a small flag will appear next to your cross hair when you hover over geometry that includes a constraint. Clicking on that geometry will load the associated Constraint Bar.

The Auto Constrain button at the left of the Parameters tab of the Ribbon will cause AutoCAD to take its best guess about what you want constrained. Clicking the diagonal arrow at the bottom of either the Geometric or Dimensional panels in the Parameters tab of the Ribbon will load the Constraint Settings dialog box (Image 9.2). From this dialog box you can control the settings for which types of Geometric

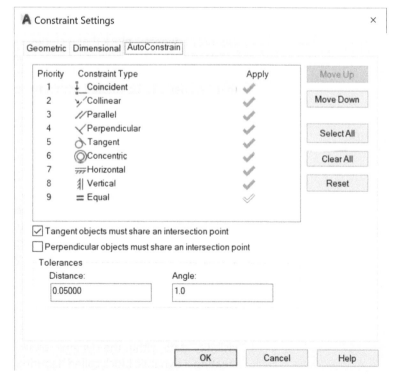

and Dimensional constraints are available. Additionally, from the Auto Constrain tab of this dialog box, you can control which constraints are used and in what priority within the Auto Constrain command. To turn a constraint off in the Auto Constrain tool, click the arrow on the right. To turn that constraint back on, click on the arrow again, turning it green. Constraints are prioritized beginning at the top of the list and working down. To change the priority of which constraints will be used, use the Move Up and Move Down buttons on the right side of the dialog box.

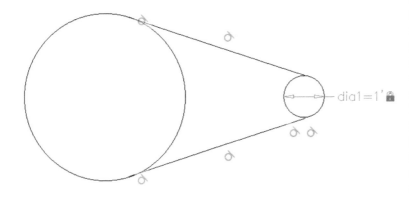

Similar to Geometric constraints, Dimensional constraints can be applied to geometry to control its size. In Image 9.3, a diameter constraint has been added to the circle on the right. Geometric constraints have also been added to keep the lines attached to the tangents of the two circles. Double clicking on the Dimensional constraint will allow you to enter a new dimension for the diameter of the circle, causing that circle to change in size. Geometric constraints applied will realign to accommodate for the new size of the circle.

Steps for Making Dynamic Blocks

For the remainder of this chapter, we will walk through the process of creating a dynamic block that includes a Visibility parameter as well as a Rotate action. A Visibility parameter allows different geometry to be visible in separate instances of the block, while a Rotate action allows that geometry to be rotated within the block. There are several other parameters and actions available within the Block Authoring palette. All follow similar methods to the Visibility parameter and Rotate action discussed below.

Plan the Block Content

Before you begin drafting, plan the items that will be included in the dynamic block. It is helpful to have a piece of scratch paper and pencil during this step. Sketch or list all items that will be included and how they will interact. When creating visibility states as we will do in our example, list out all visibility states that will be used and what will be included in each visibility state.

Draw the Geometry of the Block

Begin by creating the geometry of all items that will be included on any visibility state within the dynamic block. For our example, we will be creating a dynamic block called "Lighting" that will allow us to change between lighting instruments after inserting the block. We will begin by drawing or inserting drawings for each of the lighting instruments that we will include in our block.

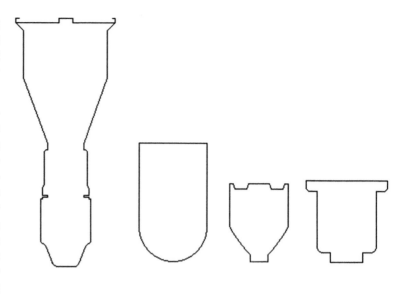

Most templates for modeling lighting instruments are readily available online through a variety of different sources. Many companies make 2D and 3D CAD models available for their lighting instruments on their website and include technical information such as weight and size. For our example of a dynamic block, we will use a set of four templates of standard theatrical lighting instruments as shown in Image 9.4.

Create Several Blocks

It is helpful at this time to create a block of each group of items that will appear in a single visibility state. For our example, we will create blocks for each of our lighting instruments and name them Light 1, Light 2, etc. Follow the steps detailed in Chapter 7 to create each of the four blocks.

While creating the blocks at this time is not necessary, it will help to organize the remainder of the process of creating a dynamic block and avoid confusion about which items belong on which visibility states.

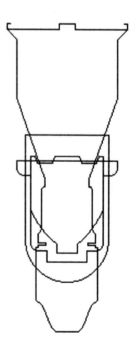

Next we will move all of the blocks so they are on top of each other in our drawing (Image 9.5). When doing this, it is helpful to place them in a position that allows the selection of an insertion point that will work for all of the individual lighting templates. For this example, we will choose the location of the C Clamp that will attach each lighting instrument to a batten.

Create the Dynamic Block

The process for creating a dynamic block is identical to that of creating a typical block. We will add the dynamic functions to the block later using the Block Editor. To begin, create a block using the Block Definition palette, exactly as we did when creating the blocks of each of our lighting instruments. For our example, we will name our new block "Lighting Instrument." We will choose our C Clamp location as our insertion point, and we will select all of the blocks we made earlier as the geometry to include in our "Lighting Instrument" block. We will also ensure that the selection box for "Open in Block editor" is selected.

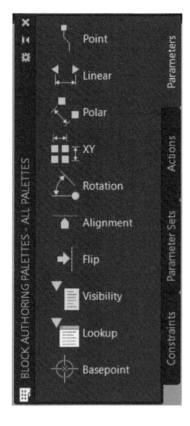

Set Constraints

If Geometric or Dimensional constraints are needed, this is the point to create them. As our lighting instruments will always be their current drawn size, there is no need to do this, so we will move on to the next step.

Set Parameters

At this point, we will set our Visibility parameter so that we can choose which lighting template is displayed based on our selection criteria. This is done using the Block Authoring palette (Image 9.6). To open this palette, navigate to the Manage panel located on the Block Editor tab of the Ribbon and click on "Authoring Palettes."

The Block Authoring palette includes tools for all actions available within dynamic blocks. For our lighting instrument example, we will be using the Visibility parameter on the Parameters tab as well as a Rotate action from the Actions tab that will allow us to rotate the lighting instrument to indicate whether it is a front light, side light or back light.

Create Visibility States

Insert a Visibility parameter by clicking on the Visibility button within the Parameters tab of the Block Authoring palette. Next, click on screen within the drawing space to indicate where to place the drop-down menu for the visibility selection to appear on screen. This drop-down menu will remain in a position relative to the block geometry whenever the block is inserted. Typically it is put to the side of the block geometry, but it can be placed wherever it is preferred by the user.

After inserting the drop-down menu for the Visibility parameter, you must define the visibility states within the block. This is done by accessing the Visibility States dialog box. Once a Visibility parameter has been added to the block and the selection arrow has been placed, the Visibility States button will be enabled within the Visibility panel of the Block Editor Ribbon tab. Clicking this button will load the Visibility States dialog box (Image 9.7).

Visibility State 0 is the default visibility state for all blocks. Rename this state to "Light 1" by

clicking on the name and then clicking the Rename button to the right of the menu box. Doing this highlights the name of the visibility state and allows you to type over the name.

Next add visibility states by clicking on the New button on the right side of the menu box. Clicking on the New button loads the New Visibility State menu box into the screen (Image 9.8). Type in the name for your new visibility state at this time (Light 2 is used for this example). You can now select to either make all items that are displayed visible, make all items that are displayed on screen invisible or leave the visibility as it is on the screen. For this example, leave the visibility as it is on the screen and it will be adjusted in the next step. Repeat this step to create new visibility states for each lighting instrument.

A New Visibility State   ✕

Visibility state name:

LIGHT 2|

Visibility options for new states

◯ Hide all existing objects in new state

◯ Show all existing objects in new state

◉ Leave visibility of existing objects unchanged in new state

[OK]   [Cancel]   [Help]

Edit Visibility States

Once the visibility states have been created, we can edit what items appear on each of the visibility states. This editing can happen at any time and new items can be drawn onto visibility states after the block is created.

To choose what items show on what visibility states use the Make Invisible button on the Visibility panel of the Ribbon (Image 9.9). This panel is located at the right end of the Block Editor tab. First choose from the drop-down menu, which visibility state you wish to work on. Begin with the visibility state named "Light 1." Next select all the objects you wish not to see in this visibility state. Once the items you wish to be invisible are selected, click the Make Invisible button in the Visibility panel of the Ribbon.

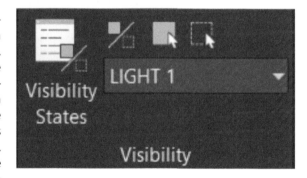

If you accidentally choose to make an item invisible that you intended to leave visible within this state, you can change the visibility mode settings to Ghost. This setting shows invisible objects so that they are drawn faintly in the background. You can then select the object you wish to make visible by clicking on the object and then clicking the Make Visible button in the Visibility panel of the ribbon.

If you spent the time to create blocks of each of the lighting instruments, you will choose which of the smaller blocks will be invisible in each state. If instead, you are attempting to select individual lines and arcs, this process can become time consuming and frustrating as it can be hard to determine which line goes with which light.

Once you have completed this process for the visibility state titled Light 1, you will need to complete the same process for each of the other visibility states.

Add Rotate Parameter

The last step in creating our lighting dynamic block is to create a Rotate parameter that will allow us to rotate the block to indicate the correct hanging position for our lighting instrument. This is a two-step process where we will first create a parameter with a base point and then add an action that will allow us to rotate our block.

This first step is to insert the Rotate parameter and select the base point for the rotation axis. To do this, click on the Rotate button within the Block Authoring palette and then click the base point for the rotation axis (in this example use the C Clamp as the rotation axis).

Next you will need to specify the radius of the Rotate parameter (Image 9.10). This is asking you to select how big the parameter will appear on your screen when you insert the block. You can either type a radius into the Command Line or extend your cursor in any direction and click to indicate the radius.

The final step in inserting the parameter is to specify the default angle for the block. This determines the angle at which the objects will appear when you insert the block. The default for this setting is 0, meaning that the objects will appear as drawn until the user specifies otherwise. If you wish to keep 0 as the default angle (typically 0 is the desired angle), you can press Enter to accept the default of 0.

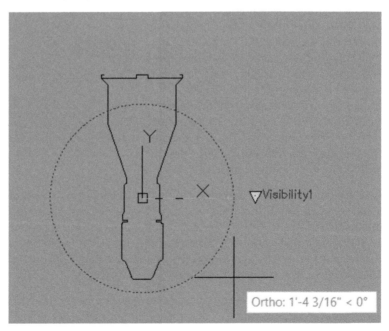

You will notice that a yellow box with an exclamation point appears next to the parameter that you have just inserted. This is to inform you that this process has not been completed and while the parameter has been inserted, there is no action associated with this parameter. Essentially, you have told the program that this is where you will want the base point for your rotation to exist, but you have not told it that you will want to rotate objects, or which objects you will want to rotate.

To finalize the Rotation parameter, you will need to associate an action with the parameter. You do this by clicking on the Rotate button from the Actions tab of the Block Authoring palette. Next choose which parameter to associate the action with by clicking on the Rotation parameter that you have just inserted, and finally select which objects you want to rotate by clicking within the drawing window or using a selection window. Press Enter to indicate that you have chosen all geometry to be included and complete the process.

At this point, the Rotation parameter will be visible on the visibility layer that it was created within and not on any others. To change this so that the Rotation parameter is available on all visibility states, toggle the visibility mode to Ghost the invisible layers, select a visibility state from the drop-down menu, select the Rotation parameter and then click on the Make Visible button. Repeat this process for each visibility state in which you wish to make the rotate parameter available.

Test and Save

You are unable to save a drawing while working in the Block Editor; however, in the top left of the Block Editor tab of the Ribbon you are able to save the block in its current state. As the Auto Save function is disabled during this process as well, it is important to remember to save when spending any substantial time creating a block. There is little worse than having the program crash after 20 minutes of work creating a dynamic block that you haven't saved since you began creating it.

Next to the Save Block button is a button that allows you to test the block. This button will allow you to try out the block and its function in a drawing window without saving the block or closing the Block Editor. When you click on the Test Block button, AutoCAD will open another drawing tab and your block will appear in a window with a slightly different color scheme. Here, all AutoCAD tools will be available and the block will act exactly as it will in a Model Space window. No work that you do in the block testing window will be saved. To exit the block testing window, click on the Close Test Block button at the right end of the Ribbon. This will return you to the Block Editor.

Once you are satisfied with the functionality of the block, click on the Close Block Editor button at the right end of the Ribbon. If you have performed any commands since you last saved the block, AutoCAD will ask you if you would like to save the changes to the block or discard the changes to the block. Select the appropriate box and the program will close the Block Editor and put you back into Model Space.

Going forward, anytime you insert this block in your drawing window, the selection boxes will appear for your defined parameters. These selection boxes appear when you first insert the block and then again when you click on the block. These selection boxes will never print when you plot a drawing.

10

EXTERNAL REFERENCES

External References are files that have been previously completed, either in AutoCAD or another software that can be loaded into a new file and viewed and/or manipulated within AutoCAD. External References can be loaded from many different file types, including other DWG files, PDFs, DWFs, images and point clouds.

External References Manager

The functionality of External References is controlled through the External References Manager (Image 10.1). To load the External References Manger type, the command XR into the Command Line and press Enter. Alternately, the External Reference Manager can be accessed through the Menu Bar by navigating to "Tools" selecting "Palettes" and clicking on "External References."

Similar to the Layer Properties Manager and other managing palettes within the program, the External References Manager can be moved around the screen, docked to the side of the screen or moved to a separate screen. To close the External References Manager, click the "X" at the top corner of the palette. All External References loaded into the drawing will remain in the drawing until commands are entered to alter this, and the External Reference Manager can be loaded at any point during the drafting process. When using several External References within a drawing, it is helpful to leave the External Reference Manager loaded and docked on a secondary screen.

Attaching External Reference Files

To attach a previously created AutoCAD file to your current drawing, click on the "Attach DWG" button at the top left of the External Reference Manger. This will load the Attachment menu (Image 10.2). While the most common file type to load into AutoCAD is other DWG files, other file types are available as well, such as DXF and PDF.

Once you have selected which type of file you would like to load as an External Reference into this drawing, AutoCAD will load a File Explorer window. Use this window

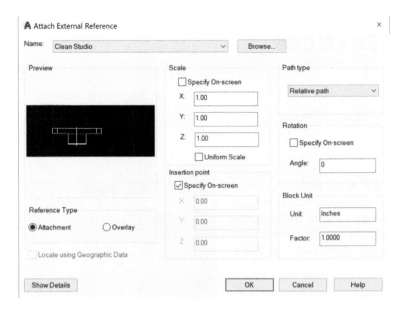

to navigate to the file you wish to load and click on that file. Once you have selected the file, the Attach External Reference toolbox will load (Image 10.3).

Within this menu, you will need to select the insertion scale. When attaching another DWG file as an XREF, the scale is usually 1:1. If you are inserting PDFs or other files the scale can be set accordingly. In this case, a scale factor can be based on the architectural scale of a drawing. To scale a 1/4" scale drawing to full size, a scale factor of 48 would be used.

Specify the rotation angle (typically 0) and the insertion point. Within theatrical drafting, it is standard to leave the intersection of the Plaster Line and the Center Line of the state at 0,0. This allows us to use 0,0,0 as the insertion point for External References, ensuring that they appear in the correct spot on the drawing screen.

You will also need to select whether this External Reference will be an attachment or an overlay. This choice affects the way that the External References contained within the current drawing will act if the current drawing is externally referenced into another drawing. Attached External References will follow the current drawing and appear within the drawing any time it is opened, either as a stand-alone drawing or when it is externally referenced within another drawing. Overlays will only appear when the current drawing is open as a stand-alone and will not appear if the current drawing is externally referenced into another drawing.

External Reference Shortcut Menu

Once an External Reference has been loaded into a drawing, you can access a shortcut menu in the XREF manager to change the behavior of the reference. To access this menu (Image 10.4) click on the name of an External Reference from the list in the XREF manager. Once the name of the External Reference is highlighted, quickly right-click on your mouse to load the Shortcut menu. The menu shown here is for an externally referenced DWG file. The menu for other file types will appear differently and have options specific to those file types.

Open

Choosing open from the Shortcut menu will open the External Reference drawing in a new window. This will allow you to make changes to the geometry of this file.

Attach

Reopens the Attach External Reference menu box.

Unload

Removes the geometry of this file from the drawing screen. The file is still attached, but is not visible and is not processed when the file is unloaded.

Reload

Reloads an unloaded file. It also is used to update the geometry in the referenced file once it has been changed in another window.

Detach

Removes the externally referenced file from the drawing.

Bind

This option exists only for externally referenced DWG files. It turns the externally referenced file into a block within the current drawing. Once an External Reference has been bound to the drawing, any changes made will only exist as a block within the current drawing and will not update the original file that had been externally referenced.

XREF Type

Allows you to change the externally referenced file to either an attachment or an overlay.

XREF Paths

The bottom three selections allow you to manage the file path that the software uses for loading the externally referenced files.

Using the full path for an externally referenced file will cause AutoCAD to use the save location of the current drawing and the save location of the externally referenced drawing to load the XREF. Changing the save location of either drawing will cause the XREF link to become broken. A relative path, on the other hand, is a partially specified folder path that does not include the drive letter or the folder of the host drawing. Using a relative path for externally referenced files allows you to move a set of drawings from your current drive to a different drive that uses the same folder structure. Relative file paths should be used when files are being shared with others through a network or cloud. Choosing "No Path" will cause no file information to be saved for the externally referenced file. When "No Path" is chosen, AutoCAD will search for the file name, beginning first with the folder that the current drawing is saved within and then through the AutoCAD support files.

Choosing "Select New Path" will load a File Manager window that allows you to redefine the save location for the externally referenced file. Similarly, "Find and Replace" will load a dialog box the shows the current save location at the top and allow you to specify the new save location below.

Broken XREF Links

When you use External References within AutoCAD, the file path that you chose when you first loaded the externally referenced file into the drawing is what the program will use to look up and display the geometry on the screen. That means that if the file is deleted or moved, you will end up with a broken XREF link on your screen.

When this occurs, you will need to redefine the save location for the externally referenced file in relationship to the host drawing. To do this, highlight the file in question in the upper half of the XREF manager. The details for this file will appear in the lower half of the manager. Click on "Save Path" in the details so that the file save location is highlighted. Click on the three ellipses (…) at the right of the save location. This will load a File Manager folder that allows you to redefine the path of the file so that it will function properly.

Manipulating External References

When working with External References, there are several options for changing the geometry within the drawing that is being externally referenced. Any geometry you change within the externally referenced file will be changed in all occurrences of the file, in this drawing or others.

Opening the externally referenced file from the Shortcut menu will load a new window with the geometry of the file. You can use this window as you would for an individual drawing file to update, delete and create new geometry. Once you are finished with this process, you will need to reload the externally referenced file into the drawing to update the changes.

You can also use the Refedit toolbar. This is the same toolbar that can be used for editing block references within a drawing. To navigate to the Refedit toolbar, select Tools from the Menu Bar, hover over "Tool-Bars" then hover over "AutoCAD" and finally navigate to and click on "Refedit." Using the Refedit toolbar will allow you to make changes only to the reference that you select. When using the Refedit toolbar, all AutoCAD commands are available except for the ability to create blocks and arrays.

Clipping External References

The ability to load and unload externally referenced files is helpful in keeping a clean and organized drawing screen. When loading in large files as External References, the program can slow down and extend the drafting time required as you wait for commands to complete and updates to save. Layers that External References exist on can be frozen to relieve the systems memory when the External Reference is not in use. Additionally, a clipping boundary can be used with an External

Reference to erase unneeded geometry from the screen. These boundaries are called Xclips.

To create an Xclip, first load an External Reference into your drawing. Type the command XCLIP into the Command Line and press Enter. The Command Line will ask you to Select Objects. You will select the External Reference you wish to create a clipping boundary on either by clicking on the reference or using a selection window and then pressing Enter. Your Command Line will then load the following options (Image 10.5).

As you have not created a clipping boundary at this point, you must first create a new boundary. As New Boundary is the default, you can press Enter at this point. You now have the following options for creating an Xclip Boundary. Remember, you can type the letters highlighted in blue and press Enter to select between the options provided in the Command Line or click on them with the cursor.

Select Polyline

Allows you to select a previously drawn polyline to use as a boundary for an Xclip.

Polygonal

Allows you to draw a polygon (closed polyline) to use as a boundary for an Xclip.

Rectangular

Allows you to select two opposite corners of a rectangle to use as a boundary for an Xclip. (This is the default.)

Invert Clip

Allows you to invert the boundary of the Xclip, showing all geometry that exists outside of the boundary and hiding all geometry that exists inside of the boundary. If you wish to invert the clip, you must first type I into the Command Line and press Enter, and then proceed with drawing the boundary.

Turning On/Off Xclips

Once you have created your Xclip boundary, AutoCAD will erase the geometry outside of the boundary to create the clipped External Reference on your screen. This geometry still exists but will not appear on the drawing screen when the Xclip is turned on.

To toggle on and off a clipping boundary type XCLIP into the Command Line. You will be prompted to select the objects you wish to work with. Select the boundary you wish to turn off. Next the Command Line will prompt you to type OFF and press Enter to turn the Xclip off or ON and press Enter to turn it back on.

W Blocks

Whereas External References allow the user to load previously created drawings into a new file, the creation of W Blocks allows the user to take geometry created within the current file and write it to a separate drawing file.

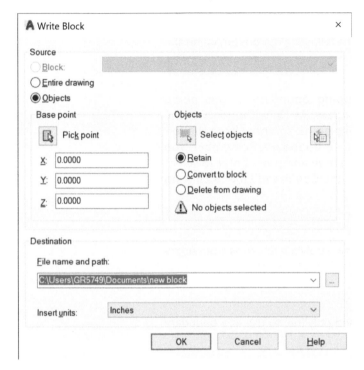

To create a W Block, type the command WBLOCK into the Command Line and press Enter. This will load the Write Block dialog Box (Image 10.6).

Here you will have the option to select which objects you wish to include in the W Block. If you choose the Objects selection, you will need to click or use a selection window within Model Space to select which objects will be included in the W Block. If you choose "Block," you will need to use the drop-down menu to navigate to the block you wish to make into a W Block. There is also the ability to W Block the entire drawing.

Once you have selected which objects will be included in the W Block, you will need to determine a base point. This base point will be used as the insertion point anytime this new file is externally referenced into any other drawing.

You will also need to determine what happens to the geometry included in the W Block upon the completion of the command. You can choose to retain the objects in their current state, convert the selected objects to a block or to delete the geometry from the current drawing.

Once you have determined what objects will be included and what will happen to them at the completion of the W Block process, you need to tell the program where to save the new drawing and what to call it. Clicking the three ellipses (...) in the file name and path area of the toolbox will open a File Explorer window. Navigate to the place that you want to save the new file to on your computer and give it a name. Once this has been completed, click OK to complete the W Block process.

Sending Drawings with External References

When sending DWG files via email, it is easy to end up with broken External Reference links. If files are saved to the hard drive of your computer, and you only send one file, those receiving that file will not have access to any included externally referenced files.

Many companies that have several draftspersons working on the same set of drawings insist that files are saved to the company network using relative paths to ensure that everyone who needs it can have access to that particular set of drafting. Within an educational or theatrical institution, there usually is not the ability or need to create a shared network to host these files. Instead we use one of the following two methods to prevent broken links.

Bind External References

DWG files included as External References can be bound to the drawing. Binding an externally referenced DWG file converts that file to a block within the current drawing. This prevents changes made in the original file from appearing in the new block and vice versa. It does, however, allow you to send an email with all geometry that was created without losing any due to broken External Reference links.

To bind all External References, open the External Reference Manager and select all External References by selecting the top External Reference in the list, navigating to the bottom of the list and selecting the bottom reference listed while holding down the Shift button on your keyboard. Once all External References on the list are highlighted, right-click on your screen and then choose "Bind" from the Shortcut menu.

Only DWG files can be bound to the drawing. If a file contains other file types as External References, you will need to create an E Transmit file to ensure that all External References are included.

E Transmit

Using the ETRANSMIT command creates a zipped folder containing the current drawing and all files that have been externally referenced into it. This allows the receiver of the file to view and manipulate the drawing exactly in the way that it was created.

Entering the command ETRANSMIT into the Command Line and pressing Enter will load the Create Transmittal dialog box (Image 10.7). This toolbox will show you a breakdown of all files being sent as well as providing an area to enter brief notes

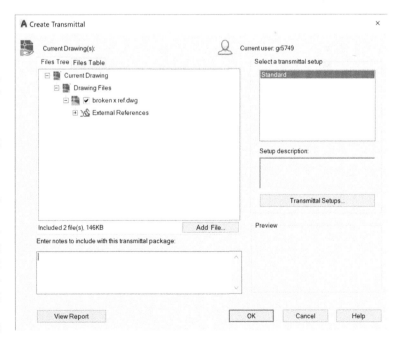

that will accompany the zipped folder. More experienced users may wish to experiment with the transmittal setup options, but the standard option is almost always sufficient. Once you click OK at the bottom of the toolbox, a File Explorer window will open. Here you will define where to save the zipped folder and what it will be called. Once the zipped folder is created, it can be sent via email or saved to an external hard drive.

11

EXPLORING PAPER SPACE

To this point of the text, we have discussed how to use the program to create and edit two-dimensional drawings of theatrical elements within Model Space. Here, objects are drawn at their actual size. It would be impossible to print out these drawn elements at their full size. The paper required would be of a ridiculous size, and a printer doesn't readily exist that would allow for this. Instead, as we do with hand drafting, we print and plot our drafting to scale. This is most easily accomplished through the use of the Layout tabs at the bottom of your AutoCAD window. These Layout tabs are commonly known as Paper Space.

Layout Tab vs. Model Tab

There are a series of tabs located at the bottom left-hand corner of your drawing window titled "Model" and "Layout 1" "Layout 2," etc. (Image 11.1). Clicking on one

of the Layout tabs will take you to a new window within the program. On this window, there is a rectangle drawn within the program and within that rectangle there is a window that allows you to view objects drawn within Model Space.

It is helpful to think of each Layout tab as a separate sheet of paper. It is within these Layout tabs that you can set up the size of the paper you will be printing on, set the outlines of the printable areas of your paper, insert title blocks and reference lines, set objects within Model Space to a specified scale and dimension and notate these objects. It is also helpful to know that nearly all the drawing and modifying commands that we have discussed to this point in the text can also be used within the Layout tabs. These objects can often be used as tools as you set up your printable areas. However, whereas objects drawn in Model Space can be set to be printed at a defined scale, objects drawn within Paper Space will print at their actual size.

Prior to defining the settings for your Layout tab, it is helpful to insert a title block to be used for defining paper size and print area. Inserting an existing title block into a Layout tab is done using the Block Insertion tools discussed in Chapter 7.

Layout Right-Click Menu

Hovering over one of the Layout tabs (either within Model Space or Paper Space) and then using a short right-click, will bring up a right-click menu (Image 11.2) that will allow you to perform several functions to manipulate the Layout tabs.

| New Layout |
| From Template... |
| Delete |
| Rename |
| Move or Copy... |
| Select All Layouts |
| Activate Previous Layout |
| Activate Model Tab |
| Page Setup Manager... |
| Plot... |
| Drafting Standard Setup... |
| Import Layout as Sheet... |
| Export Layout to Model... |
| Dock above Status Bar |

Creating New Layout Tabs

Within the right-click menu, there are several options for creating new Layout tabs. Clicking the "New Layout" button within the shortcut menu will create a new blank Layout that has the same appearance as the original Layout viewed upon first opening the program. To prevent the need for setting up a Layout tab each time you use Auto-CAD, template files can be saved that have information already included, such as paper size, a title block already inserted and plot styles and pen assignments already selected. You can also use the "From Template" button to choose to import a Layout from the template drawing of your choice. Saving a template with Layout tabs configured, title blocks inserted and styles defined can save hours of repetitive work in future drafting.

Deleting Layouts

From the right-click menu, you can also choose to delete a selected Layout. Deleting a Layout will delete all information contained within that Layout. It will not delete items drawn in Model Space that are viewed in Paper Space, but will delete any objects drawn within the Layout tab, including dimensions and annotations, title blocks, etc.

Renaming Layout Tabs

Within this menu there is also an option to rename the Layout tabs. This is often helpful as you are allowed to rename these tabs to almost anything, and using descriptive titles can save you time later if you are looking for a particular drawing within the file. Double-clicking with your mouse on the Layout name prior to entering the right-click menu will also highlight the name of the Layout and allow you to rename it by typing over the current name.

Moving and Copying Layout

Prior to entering the right-click menu if you left-click and hold on a Layout tab, you can drag it to a new position before or after other Layout tabs. This can also be accomplished through the Move or Copy dialog box (Image 11.3) that is accessed through the Layout right-click menu. Accessing the Move or Copy menu allows you to move a particular Layout before other Layouts, or to move it to the end of the list. Clicking the "Create a copy" box at the bottom of this menu will leave the original Layout in its current position while putting an

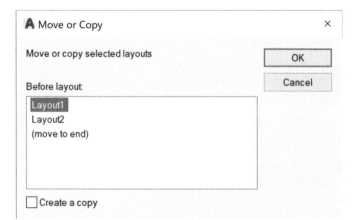

exact copy of that Layout in the new position chosen. When a copy of a Layout is created, all objects drawn on that Layout, including Model Space windows, dimension objects, title blocks, etc. are copied with the Layout to its new position.

Customizing Appearance of Sheet Layouts

As with most things within the AutoCAD software, the appearance of the Layout is extremely customizable. The most common thing that users change is the background color and the paper color that is displayed within the program; however, the Color menu that allows for these changes allows for many other changes as well.

Changing the colors in Paper Space is done using the same process used to change the colors in Model Space. To access the Color menu type "OPTIONS" into the Command Line and press Enter or click on the AutoCAD Menu in the top left corner of the screen and select "Options." Navigate to the Display tab of the Options dialog box and select the "Colors" button, which is located about halfway down on the left-hand side of the menu. This will load the Drawing Window Colors dialog box (Image 11.4). Select Sheet/Layout on the left of the dialog box and select "Paper Background" under "Interface Element." Click on the arrow under Color to change the color of the paper background. The Paper Background selection changes the color of the Paper Space drawing area everywhere but within the printable area, while the Uniform Background changes the color only within the printable area.

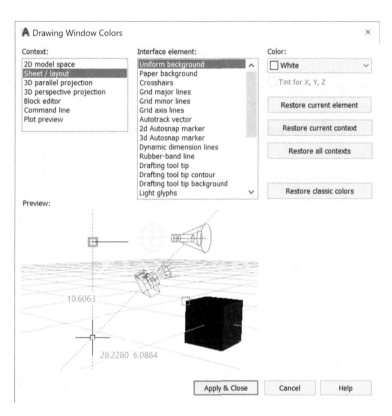

Page Setup Manager

Before laying in drawings from Model Space, setting up and including dimensions and notations and preparing to print your drawing, you need to give the program information about the size of the paper, the printer you are using and what areas within the Layout tab you wish to print. All of this is done by modifying the default page setup through the Page Setup Manager.

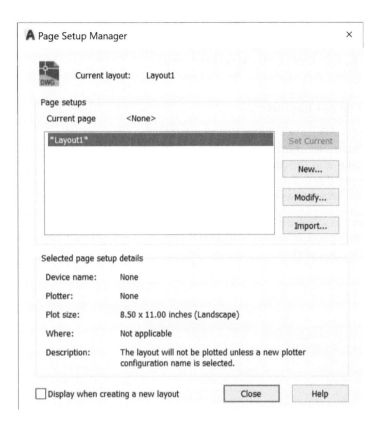

To access the Page Setup Manager, right-click on a Layout tab and select "Page Setup Manager" from the right-click menu. This will load the Page Setup Manager dialog box (Image 11.5). This dialog box includes information about what device the page is set to print to, the plot size of the sheet of paper and other information. If you wish to change any of these settings from their default, click on the name of the Layout, ensuring that it is highlighted, and then select the "Modify" button located to the right of the Page Setup Manager. This will load the Page Setup menu for that individual Layout (Image 11.6).

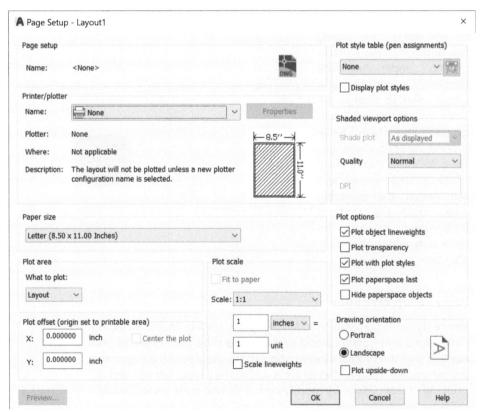

Plotter Selection

Within the Page Setup menu, you can select what plotter or printer you will be using to print the sheet Layout. Doing so will restrict the paper sizes that are available to the paper sizes that your device is capable of printing. Leaving the plotter set to the default of "None" will allow access to all paper sizes. There is also an option within the printer/plotter selection to plot drawings as PDFs, which can be shared digitally.

Paper Size Selection

Within the Page Setup Manager, you select the size of paper that you plan to print. This is fundamental to setting the scale of drawings, and knowing what can fit within a page. The list of paper sizes available within AutoCAD is extensive and fairly all inclusive. Perhaps the most important part of selecting a paper size is making sure that you have a printer capable of plotting that size paper.

Plot Area

The Plot Area allows you to define the area of Paper Space that should be printed. There are four options available within the menu under "What to Plot." Display and Extents are not frequently used. Choosing Layout will tell the program to print the default area based on the paper size selection. This is the option to choose when printing a sheet in Paper Space that has a pre-determined size.

The Window option allows you to define the printable area of the Layout tab. When you first select the Window option, you will be put back into the Layout tab to define the printing window. This is done by clicking on two diagonal corners of the printable area (such as the title block). Once you have defined the printing window, a button with the word Window< will appear under the Plot Area section of the dialog box. Clicking this button will allow you to redefine the printing window of the Layout tab. When using a Window selection to define the printable area, selecting "Center the plot" will allow that window to be centered within the printable area of the page.

Plot Style Tables (Pen Assignments)

Plot Style Tables determine what color, line type and line weight are used when printing from AutoCAD. AutoCAD comes preloaded with several Plot Style Tables. It is also possible to create and save your own Plot Style Tables.

There are two types of Plot Style Tables: color dependent and named. Color-dependent plot styles determine print settings based on what index color objects are drawn, while named plot styles allow you to assign a plot style to an object or layer regardless of color. Objects that are drawn on colors not included in the index colors (using true color or color books) cannot be mapped using color-dependent Plot Style Tables and will print at the color and line weights included in their object properties.

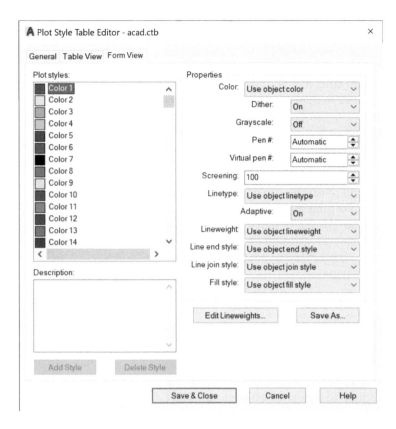

To choose from one of the preloaded Plot Style Tables that come installed with the software, click on the arrow under Plot Style Tables and choose from the list provided. None is the default and will cause your drafting to print as it is displayed on the screen. Acad.ctb is a Plot Style Table that essentially duplicates "None"; printing objects at the color and line weights defined in their layer and object properties. Monochrome defaults to printing all objects in black ink, while grayscale will print geometry as shades of gray depending on the color of the object. To load the Plot Style Table Editor for a preloaded plot style, select the plot style and click on the button to the right of the menu (Image 11.7). Here you can view and make changes to the Plot Style Table. Note that changes are only made for the color highlighted on the left of the box. Settings include line type, line weight, as well as end and connection geometry. The default for these settings is to use the object properties. Changing this will overwrite the object properties in the printing process. If changes are made to an existing color-dependent Plot Style Table, it is recommended that you perform a "Save As" and save the new Plot Style Table with a new name. Clicking "Save and Close" will overwrite the existing Plot Style Table.

To create a new Plot Style Table, navigate to the AutoCAD menu in the top left corner of your screen, hover over "Print" on the left side of the menu, and on the right scroll down and click on "Manage Plot Styles." This will load a Windows File Manager in the location where Plot Style Tables are saved. To create a new Plot Style Table, double-click on "Add-a-Plot Style Table Wizard." The Wizard will walk you through the process of creating a new Plot Style Table, either from scratch or using an existing plot style as a starting point.

If you choose a color-dependent plot style, 255 plot styles will be loaded (one for each index color) and you will need to define the plot style for each index color. If you choose to create a named plot style, a new Plot Style Table will be created with one plot style named "Normal." You will then be able to create new named plot styles using the Plot Style Table Editor. To add plot styles to the named Plot Style Table, click on the "Plot Style Editor" button prior to clicking "Finish" on the setup Wizard.

Objects can be set to print to the named plot style in their object properties. Additionally, all objects on a given layer can be set to print to a named plot style in the Layer Property Manager.

Plot Scale

The Plot Scale option controls the final size of the printed paper. Checking "Fit to Paper" will stretch or shrink the drawing so that it fits on the paper size defined. Similarly, changing the scale of the printed page will stretch or shrink the drawing on the printed page.

Setting the scale of objects drawn in Model Space is done using Viewports (discussed below). Changing the plot scale will change the size of the entire sheet of paper, and objects set to scale within Viewports will not be printed to their defined scales. A plot scale of 1:1 is most commonly used and ensures that drafting prints at the scales you define.

Plot Options

There are a series of boxes that can be checked or unchecked that control the print quality, the amount of ink and processing speed of the program as it plots drawings. Ensure that "Plot Object Lineweights" and "Plot with Plot Styles" are checked to ensure that the settings you have defined are transferred to the printed page.

Plot Orientation

The final area to control in the Page Setup Manager is to define which direction the page should print, portrait or landscape. Typically, pages for theatrical drawings are printed in landscape orientation with the wide side of the page running from left to right; however, there are occasions when a portrait-oriented drawing is appropriate.

Viewports

A Viewport, or Model View, is a window placed within a Layout tab that allows you to view geometry that exists within the Model Space tab. Objects drawn at full size in Model Space can be viewed and set to a specific scale in Paper Space through the use of Viewports.

Viewports can be created through the use of the Model View command. Additionally, geometry created in a Layout tab can be converted into a Viewport.

To create a Viewport, while in a Layout tab type the command MV into the Command Line and press Enter. Optionally, to access the command through the Ribbon, click on the Layout tab on the Ribbon, and navigate to the "Layout Viewports" panel (Image 11.8).

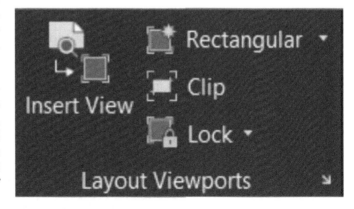

The default shape for a Viewport is a rectangle, which means that once you enter the command via the shortcut, you can select two diagonally opposite corners of the Viewport you wish to draw, and a Viewport will be drawn accordingly. Other options for drawing Viewports are to create a polygonal Viewport, or to select a previously drawn object to be used as a Viewport. To set an object as a Viewport, it must be a closed polygon, or a closed circle. This allows the program to define the closing points of the Viewport.

Drawing Multiple Viewports

Within the command for creating Viewports exists a subcommand that allows you to draw multiple rectangular Viewports at one time. To access this subcommand, enter the Viewport command and choose 2, 3 or 4 from the subcommand menu. If you choose 4, the program will automatically draw four equal sized Viewports that are drawn in quadrants of the rectangle you define. Choosing 2 or 3 will enter you into another subcommand that will allow you define the position of the Viewports. Two Viewports can either be drawn next to each other left and right or on top of one another. Three Viewports can also be drawn in similar fashion and are defined through the subcommand as well.

Activating Viewports

Once a Viewport is drawn into the Layout, you will need to place the appropriate objects from Model Space into the Viewport. To do so, double-click inside of the Viewport to activate it. This will insert your cursor into Model Space through the Viewport. If you were to draw any objects at this time, they would actually be drawn in Model Space instead of Paper Space. A button on the Function Bar will say either "MODEL" or "PAPER" depending on which window your cursor is set to. To change the space you are in, you can either double-click outside of the Viewport to get back into Paper Space or click the MODEL/PAPER button to change back and forth between spaces. Additionally, you can use the keyboard shortcut PS, which will close the Viewport and return you to Paper Space.

With your cursor in Model Space, you can zoom and pan around Model Space to find the objects that you wish to place within the Viewport for printing.

You will need to isolate only the objects you wish to see in this particular view within a Viewport. Using the Layer tool "Freeze in Viewport" will allow you to freeze a layer only within the activated Viewport. Layers frozen with this tool will still be visible in both Model Space and within other Viewports.

Scaling and Locking Viewports

Once the objects you wish to print are set into a Viewport, it is necessary to set these objects to a defined scale. When a Viewport is activated, the appearance of the Function Bar at the bottom right of the screen changes to include commands that control Viewports (Image 11.9).

When a Viewport is acti-
vated or when it is not acti-
vated but it has been selected within the sheet Layout, the drawing
scale of the objects within those Viewports is displayed within the
Function Bar. To change the scale of these objects, click on the current
scale in the Function Bar. This will load a menu with a list of predefined
standard scales. Select the scale that you wish to use for printing the
objects. Note that using the scroll wheel to zoom within an activated
Viewport will change the scale of the objects within the Viewport.

Next to the scale setting in the Function Bar when a Viewport is selected
is the icon of a pad lock. This icon allows you to lock and unlock Viewports. Locking a Viewport prevents you from changing the scale of
objects in that Viewport, as well as preventing you from panning or
zooming in Model Space within that Viewport.

Once the page setup has been defined, a title block has been inserted
and objects are set to scale within Viewports, the final step before
printing is to add dimensions and notes to your drawing.

12

DIMENSIONS AND NOTATIONS

Dimensions and notations are entered using the Annotation tools contained within the Annotate panel of the Ribbon. Notes can be entered into a drawing using the Text tools discussed in Chapter 7. Standard Text entered into a Layout tab will print at the height defined in the Text Style. Dimensions are entered using a series of tools contained within the Annotate panel of the Ribbon.

Dimension Style

Prior to adding dimensions to your drafting sheet, you will need to first define the dimension style that you wish to use when doing so. Just as you must set your drawing units and preferences before beginning to draw in Model Space, you must also define the dimension units and preferences to be used when inserting dimensions into a drawing file. This is accomplished through the Dimension Style Manager (Image 12.1).

To access the Dimension Style Manager, navigate to the Menu Bar, select the Dimension panel and click on the diagonal arrow in the bottom right corner. Alternately, use the shortcut "D" in the Command Line and press Enter.

AutoCAD comes preinstalled with two dimension styles, Annotative and Standard. Similar to the Text Style Manager discussed in Chapter 8, these dimension styles can be modified and new dimension styles can be created. Once you have defined dimension styles, they can be saved as part of a template file for use in future AutoCAD drafting.

Annotative vs. Standard Dimensions

On the left side of the Dimension Style Manager you have two choices of dimension types. Standard dimensions allow you to specify the height, style and size of dimensions, keeping those dimensions the same size no matter what. When using Standard dimensions, it is important that you only insert dimensions into Paper Space and not into Model Space. Dimensions inserted in Paper Space will print at the size defined in the Dimension Style Manager.

Standard style dimensions that are entered into Model Space will be drawn in Model Space at the size defined, and will scale accordingly when the drawing is set to scale within a Viewport. This will cause dimensions to appear extremely small and become unreadable when printed.

Annotative dimensions are set to a scale so that they appear the same when printed, ignoring the scale of the objects in the drawing. Using Annotative dimensions will allow you to place dimensions into Model Space that are sized so that they appear the same height in Paper Space. When inserting Annotative dimensions, you always insert them into Model Space; however, prior to inserting the dimensions, you must define the scale of the Viewport that the dimensioned object will be drawn within. The Annotation tools contained in the Function Bar are used to set the scale for Annotation dimensions.

While AutoCAD provides a choice to continue to add dimensions in Model Space using Annotative dimensions, the industry standard is to use Standard dimensions and to enter dimensions and notes in Paper Space.

Modifying Dimension Styles

To create a new dimension style, click the "New" button in the Dimension Style Manager. Give the new dimension style a name of your choosing. If you wish for the new dimension style to be Annotative, check the selection box, and leave the box unchecked to use a Standard dimension style.

Once you have made the appropriate selections, click continue to load the New Dimension Style dialog box (Image 12.2). The same method is used to modify existing dimension styles. To modify an existing dimension style, highlight the previously created dimension style in the list on the left by clicking with your cursor, and then select the "Modify" button on the right of the Dimension Style Manager.

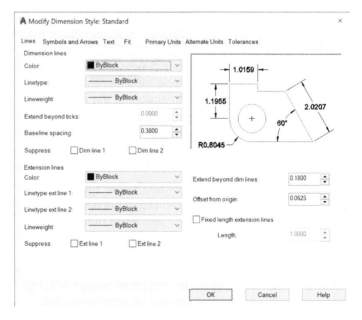

Primary Units

The Primary Units tab in the Dimension Style Manager is where you will set the units that you will use for dimensioned objects. Ensure that your dimension units match your drawing units that you set in your user preferences. For American Standard units, select "Architectural" that will provide dimensions in feet and inches. On this tab, you will also select your fractional format, and the precision of your dimensions (1/16″ is typically used for most theatrical drafting).

Zero suppression defines when a "0" is shown within a dimension line. Checking the box to suppress leading zeros will cause the dimension of 0′–9″ to appear as 9″. Suppressing trailing zeros will cause the dimension 9′–0″ to appear as 9′.

The format for giving angular dimensions also needs to be defined (decimal is used for architectural dimensions).

Lines

The Lines tab of the Dimension Style Manager allows you to define the line type and line weight of dimension lines. Once again, these can be set to "By Layer" if you choose to create a layer for your dimensions. Dimension lines are defined as the lines on either side of the dimension text.

Below the dimension line section of this tab, the Dimension Style Manager allows you to separately define the line type, line weight and color of the extension lines. Extension lines are the lines that extend from the end of the dimension line to the object being dimensioned. On the bottom right of this tab, you can specify how far the extension lines extend beyond the dimension lines as well as the offset distance, or the break between the extension line and the object being dimensioned.

As changes are made to the dimension style, the window in the top right corner of the Dimension Style Manager will update in real time to show you the changes that will be made.

Symbols and Arrows

Similar to the Lines tab of the Dimension Style Manager, the Symbols and Arrows tab allows you to customize the look of the arrows within your dimension line. It also allows you to define the look of center marks for dimensioning circles and arcs, the look of symbols used for dimensioning the lengths of arcs and jog angles for radius and linear dimensions. Changes will be displayed in the window in the top right corner of the Dimension Style Manager.

Text

The text tab of the Dimension Style Manager defines the text style used within the dimension style. At the top of the window in this tab, you can select from text styles loaded into the drawing file. You can also use the text color to overwrite the color of the text in the text style definition and use the fill color to shade the background behind dimension text. For Standard dimensions, text height is controlled by the text style being used. You can also check the box to draw a box around the dimensions text.

At the bottom of this tab, you have control over text placement and text alignment within the dimension line. As with other tabs, changes to the dimension style will preview in the window in the top right corner of the Dimension Style Manager.

Fit

The settings defined within the dimension style will be used whenever they fit on the paper. Occasionally, dimensions will not be able to fit on the paper as defined. This may occur because the object being dimensioned is too small or because other dimensions are already placed in the default location. The options within the Fit tab of the Dimension Style Manager allow you to define where dimensions will be placed when they cannot be placed in their default location.

Alternate Units

The Alternate Unit tab allows you to specify an alternate unit to be displayed in your dimensions. Using alternate dimensions will allow you to display both architectural dimensions as well as metric dimensions when necessary. Choosing the "Display Alternate Dimension" check box at the top of this tab will show both units when placing dimensions in your drawing.

Tolerance

The Tolerance tab allows you to define the upper and lower limits when placing dimensions that require precision within specific tolerances. While including tolerance dimensions is not necessary for most theatrical drafting, they can be required when creating precision machined parts.

Ribbon Annotate Panel

The Home tab of the Ribbon contains an Annotate panel that has access to some of the most commonly used Annotation tools. Additionally, there is an Annotate tab within the Ribbon that provides access to all Annotation tools (Image 12.3).

Dimensions

There are several different types of dimensions that AutoCAD will allow you to enter. When entering dimensions in a Layout tab, AutoCAD will allow the snap points from the objects shown in the Viewport to be selected so that dimensions can be placed on top of the view.

To view a list of available types of dimensions within AutoCAD, from the Home tab of the Ribbon click on the arrow next to the small dimension

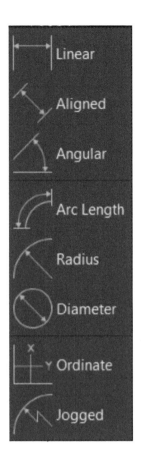

symbol in the top right corner of the Annotation panel (Image 12.4). Alternately, navigate to the Annotate tab of the Ribbon where you can use the tools within the Dimension panel.

The Smart Dimension tool (DIM) is located at the center of the Annotation panel on the Home tab of the Ribbon as well as at the left of the Dimensions panel on the Annotate panel of the Ribbon. This tool will allow you to select an object or a set of objects and for AutoCAD to take its best guess and to apply several types of dimensions based on the geometry within those objects.

A Linear Dimension (DLI) (Image 12.5) will provide a horizontal or vertical distance between two points of an object.

An Aligned Dimension (DAL) (Image 12.6) will provide the shortest distance between two points.

An Arc Length (DAR) will give you the length of an arc along the curve of the arc.

The Radius Dimension tool (DIMRAD) will provide a dimension for the radius of an arc or a circle, while the Diameter Dimension tool (DIMDIA) will provide the diameter of an arc or circle, such as the size of a hole to be drilled.

The length of any arc or polyline arc segment can be measured using the Arc Length (DAR) dimension tool.

Ordinate Dimensions allow you to define a base point and then to specify the horizontal and vertical distances away from that base point. Setting the intersection of the Center Line and Plaster Line as a base point in a ground plan will allow you to plot points that can be used for installation of scenery and lighting. Outside of the AutoCAD world these are known as Coordinate Dimensions.

Continuous vs. Baseline Dimensions

Two dimension choices that save significant time in the dimensioning process are Continuous and Baseline dimensions. A Continuous dimension (Image 12.7) allows you to select a start point and an end point for a Linear dimension, and then to use the end point of the first dimension as the start point for the following Continuous dimension. This is often called Chain dimensioning in hand drafting and within other drafting software.

A Baseline dimension (Image 12.8) allows you to define dimensions to multiple points of an object from a single base point. The Baseline Dimension tool needs a based dimension to start from. This means that you need to place a Linear or Aligned Dimension first prior to entering the Baseline Dimension tool. The Baseline tool will use the base point information from the snap points selected as part of the original dimension. After entering the Baseline tool, the next point you choose will act as an end point for a second dimension.

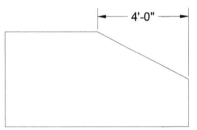

AutoCAD will continue adding Baseline dimensions each time you click on the screen until you escape the command.

Quick Dimension

The Quick Dimension tool will dimension several objects at once, but will not recognize objects set within a Viewport when dimensioning in Paper Space the way a typical dimension tool will. This means that to use the Quick Dimension tool, you must use Associative dimensions within Model Space for the dimensions to print to the correct size.

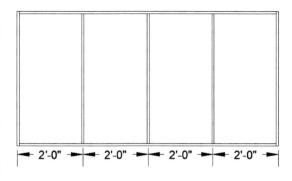

Dimension Association

When dimensions and annotation objects, such as leaders, are inserted into drawings, they are associated with snap points on the objects that they dimensioned. If the objects are changed after the dimensions have been inserted, the dimension should update to reflect the new size of the geometry.

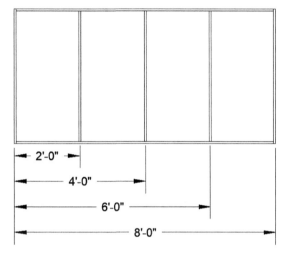

Occasionally, updating geometry after it has been dimensioned can cause the dimension to become disassociated from the geometry. When this happens, AutoCAD will place a yellow box with an exclamation point next to the disassociated dimension. Dimensions are associated based on where they are attached using the Object Snaps of the objects shown. When drawing a flat, a dimension that is attached to the endpoints or midpoints of rails, stiles and toggles will typically update to remain associated to the snap point chosen. Dimensions attached to an intersection point are more likely to break if that intersection point changes.

This disassociation of dimensions typically only occurs when plating 3D models using the Viewbase command. Sometimes, the warning that objects have become disassociated can be helpful, but it can be annoying if your entire plate is covered in yellow exclamation boxes. If you wish to turn off the Annotation Monitor, type the keyboard command ANNOMONITOR into the Command Line and press Enter and then set the value to -1 and press Enter again. This will turn off all existing warning boxes and prevent the program from providing further warnings about disassociated objects.

Leaders and Multileaders

Leaders can be used to point out specific details and to call attention to features within a drawing. Similar to Text and Multiline text, there are two types of leaders that AutoCAD recognizes; a Quick Leader (QL) and a Multileader (MLD). A Quick Leader will draw an arrow with a single

QUICK LEADER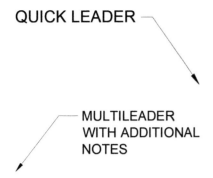

MULTILEADER
WITH ADDITIONAL
NOTES

line and allow you to enter a single line of text (Image 12.9). A Multileader will allow you to insert multiple lines of text on a Leader Line, with the first line of text existing on top of the Leader Line and the remaining lines aligned below the Leader Line (Image 12.10).

Prior to inserting Quick Leaders and Multileaders, you will need to define the leader style using the Multileader Style Manager (Image 12.11) in a similar fashion to setting the dimension style prior to inserting dimensions. To access the Multileader Style Manager, either select the small diagonal arrow at the bottom right of the Leader panel within the Annotation tab of the Ribbon or type the shortcut command MLS into the Command Line and press Enter.

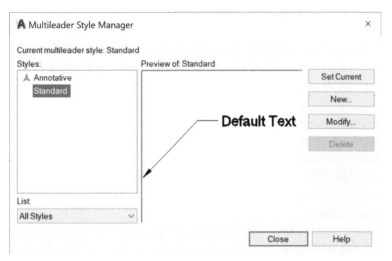

To create a new Multileader style, select the "New" button on the right side of the window, give the new style a name and select continue. To modify an existing Multileader style, select the name of the style you wish to change, ensuring it is highlighted, and select the "Modify" button on the right. Similar to dimensions, Multileaders can be assigned to be Annotative or Standard.

Within the Multileader Style Manager, leaders can be set to be straight with a defined number of points, or defined as a spline. There are also options for line weights, text size, position of the leader landing point and where text is placed on the leader landing point. Many of these options can be set to "By Layer" if you choose to create a layer for your dimensions or leaders.

As with other styles in AutoCAD, Multileader styles can be saved to a template drawing preventing the need to recreate them each time you draft.

Tables

The Table tool in AutoCAD allows you to insert a table within an Auto-CAD window. To create a table from scratch, navigate to the Annotate tab on the Ribbon and select the "Table" button within the Table panel. This will open the Insert Table dialog box (Image 12.12) where you can design the size, look and function of the table. There are also more advanced options within the Table panel that allow you to extract data from attributed blocks, export data and import data from other files and to create data links with an Excel spreadsheet.

Table Styles can also be predefined and saved as part of a template drawing using the Table Style Manager (Image 12.13). To access the Table Style Manger, either click on the small diagonal corner under the Tables panel on the Annotate tab of the Ribbon or enter the shortcut TS and press Enter. From here you can modify the existing table style or create new table styles.

From the Table Style Creation dialog box, you can control the properties of the text and the borders of the table, as well as manage the content contained within the cells of the table.

Wipeouts and Revision Clouds

Under the Markup panel of the Annotate tab of the Ribbon are two tools called Wipeout and Revision Cloud. These tools allow you to indicate changes and highlight revisions within drafting plates.

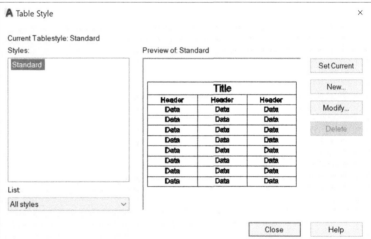

A Wipeout creates a polygonal shape that hides objects on the drafting plate. When you select the Wipeout tool, the Command Line will ask you to specify points for the Wipeout. Point your cursor on the drawing window and left-click to select the first point. You will need to select a minimum of three points to define the polygon to use as a Wipeout area.

Prior to selecting the first point of your Wipeout, the Command Line will provide the subcommand Frames. Using this subcommand, you can choose whether to display or hide the frame, or the outline, of the Wipeout. This subcommand controls only the frame that acts as the border around the edge of the Wipeout. Geometry that exists within the Wipeout will be hidden from view until the Wipeout is deleted.

Revision Clouds create cloud-shaped "bubbles" used to highlight changes in a revised drawing. AutoCAD provides three options for drawing these Revision Clouds: Rectangular, Polygonal and Free Hand. When using a Rectangular Revision Cloud, you will need to select opposite diagonal corners of the rectangle. The Polygonal Revision Cloud operates using the same method used in creating Wipeouts, while the Free Hand Revision Cloud allows you to define multiple points on the screen to define the border of the Revision Cloud.

13

PLOTTING AND PUBLISHING SHEET LAYOUTS

Once you have your drawing set with title blocks, reference lines, objects in Viewports and all necessary dimension and notation objects, the last step is to plot (or print) the drawing. AutoCAD drafting sheets can be plotted to a designated printer or plotter, or be printed to a PDF file. In addition, several sheet Layouts can be published to a single multipage PDF file.

Plotting Individual Sheet Layouts

Plotting or printing individual plates within an AutoCAD file is quite a simple task, especially if you have already completed the page setup process explained in Chapter 11. Within the Page Setup Manager, the plot area, plot style and pen assignments have already been selected, significantly reducing the steps required to plot and print the drawing.

To access the Plot menu, select the AutoCAD menu (The "A" at the top left of the screen) hover over the "Print" menu with your cursor and select "Plot" from the Print menu. Alternately, you can navigate to the Layout you wish to plot using the Layout tabs at the bottom of your AutoCAD window, right-click on the Layout tab and select Plot from the shortcut menu. You can also navigate to the Layout tab you wish to plot and type PLOT in the Command Line and press Enter to load the Plot dialog box. To see a preview of the plot before printing, select "Plot Preview" instead of "Plot." When you select "Plot" from the Print menu, the Plot window (Image 13.1) will appear. This window looks and acts similarly to the Page Setup Manager.

The Plot menu will default to include the same values that were defined in the Page Setup Manager for a particular Layout. Any values that are changed in the Plot menu will override values selected in the Page Setup Manager.

When all values are set to their desired settings, select the printer or plotter that you wish to print to. To create a PDF of the individual sheet Layout, select the DWG to PDF plotter selection from the menu. To view a preview of the drawing, click the "Preview" button at the bottom right of the Plot window. To continue with the printing process, click OK at the bottom right of the Plot window to send the drawing to the plotter.

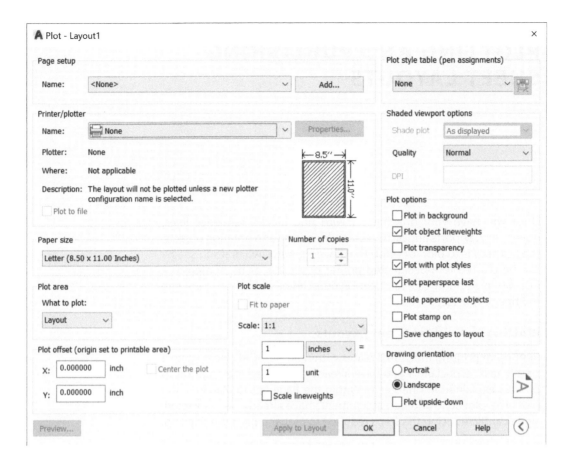

Publishing Multiple Layouts at Once

Plotting a drawing as a PDF allows you to include a single sheet Layout as a PDF file. Publishing Layouts allows you to include multiple sheet Layouts from a single drawing into a single PDF file in which each sheet Layout is included as a separate page of the same file.

To access the Publish menu, first select the Layouts that you wish to publish. Start with selecting a single sheet Layout by clicking on the Layout tab at the bottom of the screen. Use shift + left-click to select all sheet Layouts between the first sheet Layout selected and the final. Use CTRL + left-click to add or remove individual Layouts from a selection. Once all desired Layouts have been selected, right-click and select "Publish Selected Layouts" from the shortcut menu. This will load the Publish dialog box (Image 13.2). The Publish dialog box can also be accessed using the keyboard command PUB.

To send all selected Layouts to a plotter, select the "Plotter named in Page Setup" selection in the Publish To menu. To include all Layouts in a single PDF file, select the PDF selection in the same menu. Selecting the PDF option will print each sheet Layout as an individual page within a PDF viewer loaded to your computer.

Publishing several Layouts at a single time, especially from large drawing files, can take a lot of time. Standard publishing will prevent you

from any further work within the AutoCAD file you are publishing from. To prevent this delay, select the "Publish in Background" selection box at the bottom right of the Publishing toolbox. This will cause the publishing to occur in the background of the file. Publishing in the background of a file will cause the publish file to take slightly longer to produce, and will slow down the function of the AutoCAD window you are working in, but will allow you to continue to work within the file as you publish the Layouts selected.

14

EXPLORING 3D MODEL SPACE

While the ability to easily edit, copy and manipulate two-dimensional drafting is extremely helpful, the ability to complete 3D modeling sets Computer-Aided Drafting apart from hand drafting.

In two-dimensional drafting, there is a need to draft an object or scenic element several times. You need to draw a top view, a front view and a side view, plus any other views you wish to have on your printed page such as sections and details. With 3D modeling in AutoCAD, not only can you see the actual parts of a set of objects and how they interact, but you can model objects and elements a single time and use commands to plot the objects in Paper Space from different views.

Drafting quickly in three-dimensions will take some time to learn and perfect, but a skilled draftsperson will save significant time in the drafting process by drafting in three dimensions. AutoCAD provides seemingly endless options for creating 3D models, including the ability to draft surfaces and mesh, render light and shadows, include and render geographical data, etc. As this text is not intended to be an all-inclusive AutoCAD text, focus will be placed on 3D Modeling and Editing tools that are most commonly used for most theatrical drafting.

Setting Up 3D Model Space

To this point in the text, we have drawn all of our geometry in two dimensions within Model Space. As such, our UCS (User Coordinate System) has only shown us the X and Y axis on our screen. As you are aware, X is the Horizontal plane and Y is the Vertical plane. However, the Z axis has always existed in your modeling window. It is the axis that exists going in and out of the computer screen.

All of the tools for 3D modeling can be accessed within the Drafting and Annotation workspace with some user customization and the addition of toolbars. AutoCAD also has two additional workspaces, titled 3D Basics and 3D Modeling that reorganize the Ribbon, providing access to 3D Modeling tools within the Ribbon. To switch between workspaces, use the Workspace Switching tool (the gear icon) located in the Function Bar.

The 3D Basics workspace (Image 14.1) organizes the Ribbon to show tools for creating and modifying basic 3D objects. 2D Drawing and Modifying tools are also included in the Home tab of the Ribbon in the 3D Basics workspace.

The 3D Modeling workspace (Image 14.2) includes all of the tools included in the 3D Basics workspace, as well as many others, including 3D Modeling commands, Solid Editing tools and Mesh Modeling and Editing commands.

Whichever workspace you choose to use, all keyboard commands for drawing and editing both 2D and 3D objects will be available. If you will be using the 2D Drafting and Annotation workspace to complete 3D modeling, toolbars can be loaded to your workspace to provide access to 3D Modeling and Editing tools. The tools contained within these toolbars duplicate tools available in AutoCAD's 3D workspaces. As with all other toolbars, these can be loaded and unloaded into your drawing window, and moved around within the window.

The following three toolbars can be located on the Menu Bar under Tools: Toolbars: AutoCAD. The Menu Bar can be loaded and unloaded from the screen using the keyboard command MENUBAR. You will notice that there are many toolbars that are not being used. Some of the commands that will be discussed are repeated within the toolbars listed below. The use and selection of toolbars, as well as which work-space to use, are based completely on user preference. Spend some time experimenting with the toolbars listed below as well as others, and with the different workspaces to see what works best for you and your drafting style.

Modeling

This toolbar provides commands for drawing and manipulating three-dimensional shapes.

Solid Editing

This toolbar provides commands for editing the faces and edges of previously drawn three-dimensional objects.

View

This toolbar allows you to easily change to repeatable views of three-dimensional objects.

The View Toolbar

The View toolbar allows you to choose a direction from which to view your drawing screen. This toolbar is fairly intuitive and allows

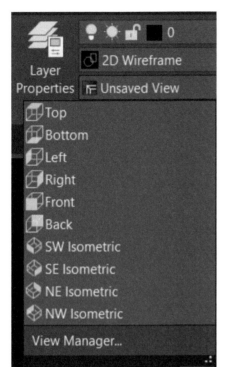

you to view Model Space in methods that are easily repeatable. There are ten wire cubes along this toolbar, each with one side highlighted in blue. Clicking on any of these cubes will automatically change your Model Space screen to view objects on the side of the cube that was highlighted. Clicking on the cube with the top highlighted blue will put you in a top view and so forth.

The commands from the View toolbar are duplicated on the Home tab of the Ribbon in both the 3D Basics and the 3D Modeling workspaces. In the 3D Basics workspace, the View commands are located under the Layers and Views panel. Click the words "Unsaved View" to load the list of available views (Image 14.6).

The same list is provided on the Home tab of the Ribbon in the 3D Modeling workspace within the View panel.

Orbit

When working with three-dimensional objects, you still have the ability to zoom and pan as you did with two-dimensional objects. Moving the scroll wheel on your mouse will zoom in and out on the drawing and holding down the scroll wheel while moving your mouse will pan around the screen.

When working with three-dimensional objects, you also have the ability to orbit the drawing using the 3D Orbit (3DO) command. This command can also be entered by holding shift on your keyboard and moving your mouse while depressing the scroll wheel on your mouse. The 3D Orbit command will orbit around all objects within the drawing window. If you wish to orbit around only a single object, you can click on that object prior to orbiting and Auto-CAD will hide all other objects on the screen and orbit around only that object.

The command 3DORBITCTR also allows you to specify a center point for the orbit by clicking on screen.

View Options within Model Space

In the top left corner of Model Space (Image 14.7), there are three toolbars that provide several more options for manipulating the view within Model Space.

[−][Top][2D Wireframe]

Viewport Controls

Within AutoCAD there are two types of devices, both called Viewports. Layout or Paper Space Viewports, discussed in Chapter 11, provide a window within a Layout tab to view objects drawn within Model Space. AutoCAD also contains a device called a Model Space Viewport. Model Space Viewports split the drawing window of your Model Space allowing you to see objects drawn in Model Space from several directions at the same time.

The minus sign all the way to the left provides access to the Viewport Controls toolbar (Image 14.8). This toolbar allows you to add several tools to Model Space that controls the views of your screen as well as how many Viewports you have on your screen at a time.

Viewport Configuration

The top option in the Viewport Controls toolbar is to "Restore Viewport." Clicking on this will split the view of your computer monitor into four separate Model Space screens. Any object drawn within one Model Space Viewport will also appear in all other screens. However, different Viewports can be viewed from different angles. Navigating to the Viewport Controls toolbar within any Model Space Viewport and clicking "Maximize Viewport" will cause that Viewport to expand to a full screen view.

Clicking on the "Viewport Configuration List" within the Viewport Controls toolbar will load a list of options to customize how many Viewports you want within your drawing window and how you wish them to be organized. For example, choosing "Four: Right" will place one large Model Space window on your screen with three smaller windows on the right of the large window.

The keyboard command VIEW-PORTS can also be used to manage your Model Space Viewports. If you dock palettes, such as the Layer or Properties Palette to the left side of your screen, the minus sign that allows access to the Model Space Viewport configuration can become hidden. Using the keyboard command will load the Viewports dialog box (Image 14.9), which duplicates the options available using the minus sign.

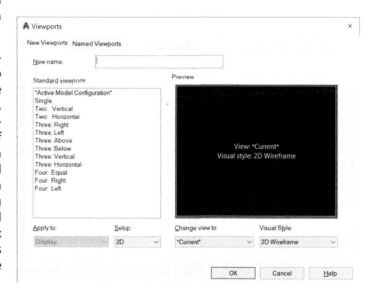

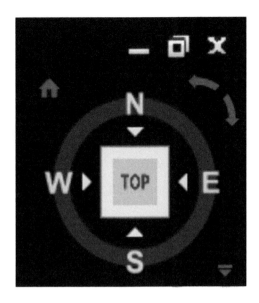

The View Cube

Under the Viewport Controls toolbar, there is the option to turn on or off the View Cube (Image 14.10). This can also be done using the View Cube button within the View tab of the Ribbon within any workspace. The View Cube duplicates many of the commands contained within the View toolbar but does so within a cube that you click on to navigate to a certain view. You can click on the arrows around the cube, on a face, edge or corner of the cube as well as the rotation arrows at the top right side of the cube. As you click on the cube, your Model Space window will orbit to match the view selected on the View Cube.

The View Cube changes only the direction that you are looking at the Model Space and not the plane on which you are drawing. Using the View toolbar to change the view of the model to a pre-defined viewing direction changes both the view of the model and the plane on which you are drawing.

When you hover your cursor over the View Cube, three additional icons appear. Clicking on the arrow in the bottom right corner will load a menu that allows you to customize the way the View Cube looks and functions. Within this menu, you can choose which view to set as your "Home" position. The View Cube settings will load a dialog box that allows you to define the display and actions used by the View Cube. You also have the ability to change what projection is used to view the drawing window.

The two arrows at the top right corner of the View Cube will rotate the model about the face currently used by the View Cube. Clicking on the icon of the house will return the model to the defined home position.

The Steering Wheel

The Steering Wheel is used more often for camera views and animation than for drawing functions. The Steering Wheel, however, does contain clickable access to the Pan, Zoom and Orbit commands. The Steering Wheel is a floating toolbar that is attached to the cursor of your mouse once you select it from the Viewport Controls toolbar. To close the Steering Wheel and remove it from your screen, click the small "x" located in the top right corner.

The Navigation Bar

The Navigation Bar (Image 14.11) provides clickable access to the Pan, Zoom and Orbit commands. The Navigation Bar also provides access to animation and 3D tour (video fly by) tools. As with the View Cube, the Navigation Bar can be turned on or off using the Viewport menu in the top left corner of the drawing window, or by navigating to the View tab

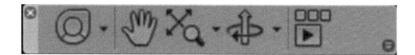

of the Ribbon in any of the AutoCAD workspaces and clicking on the button near the left edge of the screen.

Clicking on the small arrow at the bottom of the Navigation Bar will allow you to customize what tools appear in the Navigation Bar. Hovering over "Docking Position" will load a list of four options for docking the Navigation Bar. When first loaded, the Navigation Bar is linked to the View Cube, meaning that the two will move around the screen together. From the Docking Positions menu, you can unlink the Navigation Bar from the View Cube, and then move the Navigation Bar to any position on your screen that you wish.

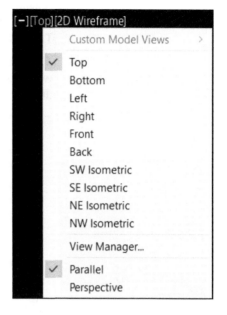

View Controls

The View Controls toolbar (Image 14.12) located next to the Viewport Controls toolbar provides a drop-down list of views. This toolbar will update to reflect the view that you are in within your Model Space window even if you are using a different tool to change views. You may also click on a view from the drop-down menu to navigate to that particular view.

Visual Styles Controls

The Visual Styles Controls toolbar (Image 14.13) allows you to change the appearance of three-dimensional objects on your screen to show them as solid objects instead of line drawings. Changing this view can be extremely helpful, especially when you are first beginning to draft in three-dimensions. It is also helpful for presentational purposes.

The Visual Styles Controls can also be accessed within the Ribbon of the 3D Basics and 3D Modeling workspaces. They are located on the Visual Styles panel within the Visualize tab of the Ribbon in the 3D Basics workspace as well as on the View panel of the Home tab of the Ribbon in the 3D Modeling workspace.

With larger drawings, the rendering power required to draft in Hidden, Shaded or other views will often exceed the ability of your computers graphic card. As you become more experienced with drafting in three dimensions, begin drafting in a 2D wireframe visual style and check your work with other visual styles as needed. This will take time to get used to, but with a little practice and a lot of patience it will save your computer processor and your graphics card, causing the program to be less likely to crash.

Manipulating the UCS

The UCS sets the origin and the orientation of the XYZ axis of your drawing window. To this point in the text, we have only used the XY axis of the UCS and it has remained at its home position of 0, 0. This home position is known as the "World" UCS position. AutoCAD allows you to move the UCS to different locations and orientations within the drawing window and to align the UCS with certain objects.

The UCS Command

Typing the command "UCS" into the Command Line and pressing Enter will load the UCS command and the several options associated with it (Image 14.14).

UCS commands are also available in the Ribbon when using either a 3D Basics or 3D Modeling Workspace setting. From a 3D Basics workspace setting, navigate to the Visualize tab of the Ribbon. The UCS commands are contained within the Coordinates panel. In a 3D Modeling workspace, the Coordinates panel is contained both on the Home tab and the Visualize tab of the Ribbon.

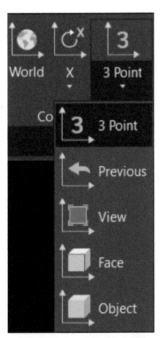

Aligning to a Face

The UCS Face command will allow you to select the face of a 3D Object (such as one of the sides of a cube) as the new home for the UCS. The UCS will align the X Y axis to sit on the selected face with the Z axis perpendicular to the X, Y Plane.

Aligning to an Object

The UCS Object command will allow you to select an object as the new home for the UCS. The UCS will align the XY axis to the object on the plane that it was originally created. The UCS Object and Face commands can be accessed by clicking on the arrow below the 3 Point command in the Coordinates panel of the Ribbon (Image 14.15).

Rotating the UCS

Selecting the X, Y or Z subcommands within the UCS command will allow you to rotate your UCS to a specified angle along the chosen axis. For example, to rotate the UCS 45 degrees along the X axis, you would enter the following commands:

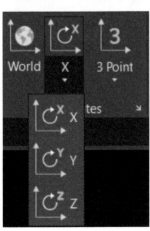

"UCS"   (press Enter)
X (press Enter)
45   (press Enter)

Similar to the Object and Face commands, the UCS Rotate commands can be accessed by clicking on the arrow underneath the X command in the Coordinates panel on the Ribbon (Image 14.16).

3 Points

The UCS 3 Points command allows you to use any three points within Model Space to define the UCS axis. The three points can be selected anywhere within Model Space, including Object Snap points, and will allow you to create a custom UCS that will allow you to cross planes in Model Space.

The UCS 3 Point command exists within the Ribbon in the Coordinates tab of either the 3D Basics or 3D Modeling workspaces. While the 3 Points command does not appear as a subcommand in the Command Line when using the UCS command, typing "3" and pressing Enter will enter you into the UCS 3 Points command.

Aligning to the World

Selecting the UCS World command will realign the UCS to its original home position at 0, 0 of your drawing window with the Z axis oriented in a top view. As this is the default subcommand within the UCS command, to re-position your UCS to its original coordinate points, type "UCS" into the Command Line, press Enter to begin the command and then press Enter to accept the default and reposition the UCS.

Origin Grips

AutoCAD also allows users to move the UCS using origin grips. Clicking on the UCS Icon will add grips at the intersection of the three axis as well as at the extension points of the UCS Icon (Image 14.17).

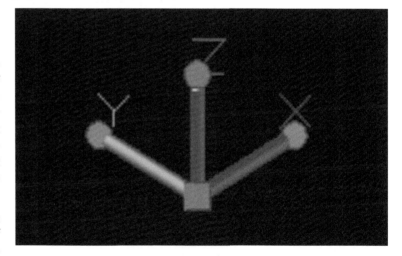

A quick left-click on the grip at the intersection of the three axis will attach the UCS Icon to your mouse cursor. A left-click elsewhere on the screen will "drop" the UCS Icon at that location repositioning the UCS.

Clicking on any one of the grips at the extension of an axis will allow you to rotate the UCS to a new orientation. It is helpful to have Orthographic mode (F8) or Polar Tracking Mode (F10) engaged to restrict your cursor to specified angles. This will avoid aligning the UCS to undesired orientations.

The keyboard command UCSICON will allow you to turn the UCS Icon on or off and define how that icon behaves on the screen. The UCS dialogue box can also be used to turn the icon on or off and to control the behavior of the UCS. To access the UCS dialog box (Image 14.18), click on the small diagonal arrow at the bottom of the Coordinates

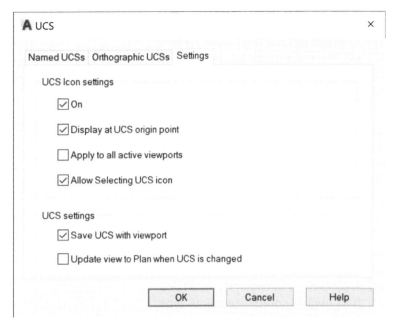

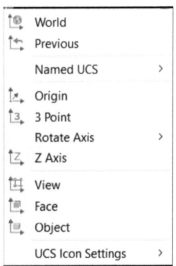

panel in the Home tab of the Ribbon within the 3D Modeling workspace. You can also access the Coordinates panel in the Visualize tab of the Ribbon within the 3D Basics workspace.

Saving a Custom UCS Origin

AutoCAD will allow you to save and recall a customized UCS origin. To do this, first position and align the UCS Icon in its desired orientation. Next, right-click on the UCS Icon to load the UCS shortcut menu (Image 14.19). Hover over the "Named" option and click on "Save" to save a new custom UCS. The Command Line will load the UCS Name command. Type the name for your custom UCS origin and press Enter to complete the command. Named UCS origins can also be created within the UCS dialog box.

To load a previously saved custom UCS origin, right-click on the UCS Icon to load the shortcut menu, hover over the "Named" option and then click on the name of the saved UCS origin.

15

3D MODELING

The Modeling toolbar and the Ribbon of the 3D Basics and 3D Modeling workspaces contain tools for drafting the most common three-dimensional objects; often referred to as primitive shapes.

The Ribbon of the 3D Basics workspace has a Create panel on the Home tab of the Ribbon that holds the tools for creating these primitive shapes. To access these tools, click on the arrow below the Box tool on the left (Image 15.1). The Ribbon of the 3D Modeling workspace duplicates this menu on the Modeling panel of the Home tab. These tools are also contained within the 3D Modeling workspace on the Ribbon under the Modeling tab within the Primitive panel (Image 15.2).

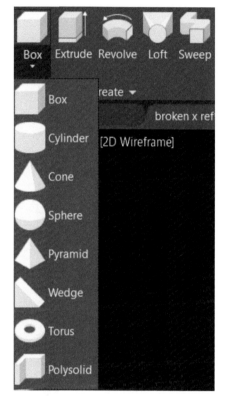

Drafting Primitive 3D Shapes

The tools for creating primitive shapes allow users to create three-dimensional objects without the need to draft two-dimensional shapes.

Box

The Box command is used to create a six-sided solid, such as a cube. After entering the Box command, either by clicking on the command in the Modeling toolbar or Ribbon or entering the keyboard command BOX you will need to select the first corner of the bottom surface of the box you will draw. After selecting the first corner, you can either select the opposite corner of that face of the box or enter the subcommands provided.

Using the Cube subcommand you can provide a dimension for each face of the cube. By definition, a cube has equal dimensions on all faces, so after entering the dimensions and pressing Enter, AutoCAD will draw the completed cube.

Entering the Length subcommand will allow you to enter a dimension for each axis of the box. As with rectangles, the length will form along the X axis, the width will form along the Y axis and the height will form along the Z axis of your User Coordinate System (UCS).

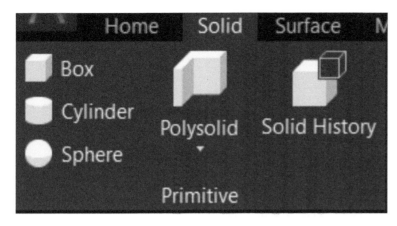

Cylinder (CYL)

To create a cylinder, enter the command, select the center point of the base of the circle, specify a radius or diameter and specify a height of the cylinder.

Cone (CONE)

After entering the Cone command, the first two steps follow the same steps for drawing a two-dimensional circle. Specify the center point of the circle by clicking on the screen. Specify the radius (or use the subcommand to specify the diameter) and press Enter. Once you have drawn the circular base of the cone, enter the dimension for the height of the cone and press Enter to complete the command.

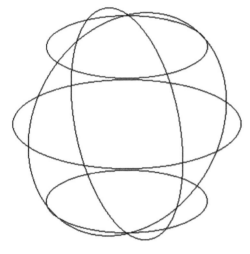

Sphere (SPH)

After entering the Sphere command, select the center point of the sphere. Next enter the radius or use the subcommand to enter the diameter and press Enter.

AutoCAD will create a sphere based upon the dimensions entered. When viewing a drawing in the 2D wireframe visual format, the sphere will appear as a set of intersecting circles surrounding a single orbit point (Image 15.3). This is a standard used by AutoCAD to differentiate the sphere from a circle. When drafting in other visual styles, the sphere only shows the intersecting lines when the object is highlighted (Image 15.4).

Pyramid (PYR)

The Pyramid command works similarly to the Cone command and the 2D Polygon command. You will need to specify the center and the radius of the pyramid. As with the 2D polygon command, you will need to specify whether the pyramid should be inscribed or circumscribed about the radius. Finally, you will need to define the height of the pyramid.

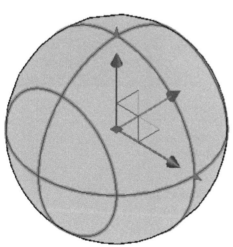

Wedge (WEDGE)

A wedge is a three-sided polyline with a defined thickness. The Wedge command works exactly the same as the Box command and includes the same available subcommands, including the cube command.

The Wedge command will automatically triangulate and connect two corners of the rectangular dimensions given to create the object. The starting point of the Wedge (the first point selected when drafting the object) will be the edge with height.

Torus

The Torus command creates a donut or tube-shaped object. You will first specify the center of the torus and then the distance from the center of the torus to the center of the tube. Next you will need to specify the radius of the tube.

Poly Solid (POLYSOLID)

It is helpful to think of a poly solid as a section of walls in your house. When drafting poly solids, you select the points of the walls on the X-Y axis of your drawing screen. You can use the subcommands within the Command Line to include arcs within your wall. All walls will have the same height and the same thickness. You can change the height and thickness of the walls using the subcommands prior to choosing the starting point of the wall.

Helix (HELIX)

The Helix (Image 15.5) is a strange drafting shape in that it is technically a three-dimensional shape as it has a dimension in all three planes, but has the thickness of a single line. Drafting a Helix alone is not often done; however, it is often used as a tool to create other more complicated shapes such as springs and spiral staircases.

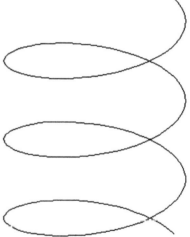

To draft a Helix, enter the command either using the keyboard entry and pressing Enter or clicking on the toolbar button. The Helix tool is contained in the slide out of the Draw panel on the Home tab of the Ribbon in both the 2D Drafting and Annotation and 3D Modeling workspaces. It is also contained in the Modeling toolbar.

After entering the Helix command, you must first specify the center point of the base of the helix and the radius or diameter of the base of the helix. Next, the Command Line will ask you for the top radius or diameter. Typically, the base of a helix will have the same radius as the top of the helix, but making them different will allow you to create a spiraling helix instead of a cylindrical helix.

After defining the radius of both ends of the helix, the Command Line will ask you to define the height of the helix. Once you define the height and press Enter, the Helix command will be completed.

Prior to entering the height in the Command Line, you have the option to choose from the subcommands in the Command Line to specify the amount of turns within the helix, or the turn height. Specifying the turn height will define the center-to-center distance between each helix turn.

After specifying the turn height or the amount of turns, AutoCAD will return to asking you for the height of the helix. Type the height and press Enter, or click on a snap point on your drawing window to define the helix height. Note that the helix height must always be defined in the Z axis. Remember, you can change the orientation of the UCS as needed to ensure the Z axis is pointing in the desired direction.

Extruding 2D Shapes into 3D Objects

Another method for drawing a three-dimensional object is to draw a two-dimensional shape and to use the Extrude command to give the shape a specific dimension on the Z axis.

All polylines, circles, lines and arcs can be extruded, but only closed shapes, such as closed polylines and circles, will result in a 3D solid being created. Open polylines, arcs and simple lines will result in the creation of a surface.

To use the Extrude command to create a 12-inch cube, begin by using the Rectangle command to draw a rectangle with dimensions of 12 inches by 12 inches. After drawing and completing the Rectangle command, use the Extrude (EXT) command to give the rectangle a height of 12 inches on the Z axis. The Extrude command is also available on the Home tab of the Ribbon in both the 3D Basics and 3D Modeling workspaces.

After beginning the command, the Command Line will ask you to select objects. Select the rectangle and press Enter to indicate that you have completed selecting objects. Selecting multiple objects will cause all objects selected prior to pressing Enter to extrude to the same thickness. Once all objects have been selected, the Command Line will ask you to specify the height of the extrusion. In the Command Line, type "12" and press enter. This will give the 12 inch by 12 inch rectangle a thickness of 12 inches making it a cube.

Polylines, including rectangles, are only able to be drawn on the X, Y axis of your drawing screen and objects will only extrude along the Z axis of your drawing screen. Because of this, it is often necessary to change the position, direction or orientation of your UCS.

There is one important subcommand available after selecting the objects to be extruded. Instead of entering the height of the extrusion, the Command Line allows you to extrude an object along a path. In theatrical drafting, the ability to extrude an object along a path will save significant time, especially when drafting moldings. If you have all of your walls in a box set drawn, you can draw a polyline along the top of the set where the crown molding would go. On one end of the polyline draft a two-dimensional section of the crown molding being used. Ensure that the section of the crown molding is a closed polyline. Enter the Extrude command, select the 2D shape of the molding as the object to be extruded, and press Enter to signify this is the only object you wish to extrude. Instead of defining a height for the extrusion, choose the subcommand to extrude along a path. Choose the polyline to extrude the section along the path of the set and your entire crown molding will now be drafted.

Manipulating Extrusions

The following commands allow you to manipulate the way objects are extruded. These commands are included in the Modeling toolbar as well as on the Home tab of the Ribbon in both the 3D Basics and 3D Modeling workspaces.

Press Pull (Press)

The Press-Pull command allows you to manipulate how objects are extruded. Using the Press-Pull command with a single closed polyline or single circle will extrude that shape into a three-dimensional object. However, before beginning the extrusion, if you offset the closed polyline to create a bounded area, you can choose both polylines and the Press-Pull command will extrude the area within the closed boundary (Image 15.6).

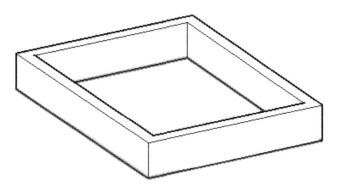

After entering the Press-Pull command, to select multiple objects, enter the "Multiple" subcommand (M) into the Command Line and press Enter. Select all the objects that you wish to extrude and press Enter to indicate your selection is complete. Then specify an extrusion height by defining the height in the Command Line and pressing Enter, or clicking to a snap point on your drawing window.

Sweep (SW)

The Sweep command works similarly to the subcommand of extruding an object along a path. Sweeping a two-dimensional object along a defined path will create a three-dimensional solid. In Image 15.7, a circle has been swept along a previously drawn helix to create a spring.

Before entering the Sweep command, you must first have drawn the two-dimensional shape to be swept and the path that it is to be swept along. Enter the Sweep command by clicking the button in the Modeling toolbar or the Ribbon, or entering the keyboard shortcut and pressing Enter. Select all objects you wish to extrude and press Enter to indicate that you are finished with your selection. Finally, click on the path that you wish to sweep the object along.

Several subcommands are available within the Sweep command. After entering the command and before selecting an object to sweep, the Mode option is available. This allows you to define whether the object will be a solid or a surface at the completion of the Sweep command.

After you have selected the object to Sweep, but before defining the Sweep path, other options are also available. The Scale option will cause the object to grow or shrink in size as it sweeps along the path. Entering a Scale of 2 will cause the object to start at its original size at the start of the sweep path and to increase in size along the sweep path until it is twice its original size at the end of the sweep path.

The Twist option will cause the object to twist along the sweep path. A twist angle of 360 degrees will cause the object to turn one full rotation along the sweep path.

When you sweep a 2D shape along a path, it is aligned perpendicular to the path. If the shape is not on the same plane as the path, the Alignment subcommand will allow you to define how the shape is aligned to the path.

The Base Point subcommand allows you to change the position where the sweep will be created. When creating a sweep, the default is to sweep the 2D profile along the path defined. This means that the 3D geometry will be created on top of the path you are using to define the shape.

Changing the base point allows you to define the point where the sweep will begin by clicking on screen, and then to use the path of the sweep to define only the shape of the geometry and not its location on the screen.

Revolve (REV)

The Revolve command extrudes an object along the perimeter of a circular path (Image 15.8). While not required, it is helpful to draw the circle that the object is to be extruded along to be used as a tool for creating the Revolve. As with other Extrusion commands, you must draw the two-dimensional shape of the object being extruded before entering the command.

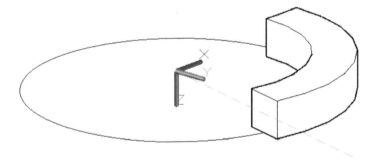

Enter the Revolve command by clicking the button in the Modeling toolbar or the Ribbon or by entering the keyboard shortcut and pressing Enter. Click on the objects you wish to extrude and press Enter to signify that you are finished with your selection. Next you will need to select the center point of the perimeter of the circle that you wish to revolve the object around. If you have previously drawn the two-dimensional circle, you can use the Center Object Snap as a selection point. You can also use construction geometry or other snap points on the screen to define the center of the revolve. After defining the center of the revolve, you will need to define the other end of the rotation axis. Ensure that Orthogonal or Polar mode is enabled to prevent errors. Click on an empty space on the screen along the axis that you wish to revolve around. Finally, you will need to specify how many degrees you wish to revolve the object around the defined center point. The default angle definition is 360 degrees. Pressing Enter will complete the object around the entire perimeter of the circle. If you wish to revolve the object less than 360 degrees, input the desired degrees in the Command Line and press Enter.

Loft

The Loft command creates a solid between previously defined two-dimensional cross sections. The more cross sections of an object that are drawn the more accurate the Loft extrusion will be to the desired object. To create a lofted object enter the Loft command by clicking on the button in the Ribbon or Modeling toolbar or by entering the keyboard command (LOFT) into the Command Line and pressing Enter. Select all cross sections that you wish to use to define the lofted object and press Enter.

Once you have selected the cross sections and pressed Enter, AutoCAD will create the lofted object. The Command Line will prompt you to enter an option to control the surface creation of the Loft. Lofted Objects have drop down windows that allow you to manipulate this surface creation. Click on the drop down menu to select the edge style of the lofted object. Once you have selected the desired edge style press Enter to complete the command. Lofted objects retain their drop down menus to allow you to change their edge styles after they have been created. To access the drop down menu after completing the Loft command, click on an object that was extruded using the Loft command. The object will be highlighted and a small arrow will appear near the object. Click on the arrow to access the menu for the lofted object.

16

MANIPULATING 3D OBJECTS

All of the tools used for manipulating 2D geometry are available for use when working with and manipulating 3D models. However, when working in three dimensions, it can be easy to move or copy an object along the wrong plane of your X, Y, Z axis. Several tools in AutoCAD allow you to define which axis of the User Coordinate System (UCS) you wish to use when manipulating objects in a 3D model.

Point Commands

Point commands allow you to move or copy objects along a single plane to a specific alignment with a snap point on another object. Using Point commands tells AutoCAD that you wish to restrict your Move or Copy commands to a single axis.

To use a Point command to move an object, enter the Move command by typing "M" and pressing Enter. Select the objects you wish to move and press Enter. Next, select your base point for moving the object. Prior to specifying the displacement point type .X .Y or .Z depending on which axis you wish to move along and press Enter. After typing the Point command and pressing Enter, click on the snap point for where you wish to move the object to and press Enter. Finally, the Command Line will ask you for the plane of the other two axis that you are not moving along. With your orthogonal mode turned on, click into space to define the plane. If you were to move an object along the X axis only, with your ortho mode turned on, you would click in space along the X axis to define the Y and Z planes as those planes would be perpendicular to the X plane.

The Point commands work both with the Move and the Copy commands. You can also use Point commands to exclude only one axis. If you wish to move or copy an object along the X and Y axis but to have it remain on the same plane in the Z axis, you can use the Point commands by typing ".XY" prior to defining the displacement point.

Gizmos

When you are using a 3D Visual style (any visual style other than 2D wireframe) and you click on a 3D object, a tool, called a Gizmo, will load at the center of the object. Three Gizmos are available to be used, the Move Gizmo, the Rotate Gizmo and the Scale Gizmo. You can also choose to not have a Gizmo appear on 3D objects.

One of the three Gizmos can be set as the default Gizmo that will appear any time you click on a 3D object. You can then toggle between the Gizmos to load the tool you wish to use. In both the 3D Basics and 3D Modeling workspaces, the Gizmo tool is located in the Selection panel on the Home tab of the Ribbon. You can also toggle between Gizmos by right-clicking on the Gizmo and selecting the Gizmo you wish to use from the shortcut menu.

The Gizmo can be relocated on the screen either by using the right-click menu or by clicking the snap point at the center of the Gizmo and dragging it around the screen with your mouse. The three axis of each Gizmo will align to the current orientation of your UCS coordinate system.

3D Move

While you can use the Move (M) command to move a 3D object, using the 3D Move command allows you to specify a single plane to move the object along. You can enter the 3D Move command by loading the Move Gizmo, clicking on the 3D Move button within the Modeling toolbar, or using the keyboard shortcut 3DMO.

If you use the keyboard command or button in the Modeling toolbar, the Command Line will ask you to select the objects you wish to move. Select the objects and press Enter. After you press Enter, the 3D Move Gizmo will appear on the objects you have selected (Image 16.1). If you are working in a 3D visual style, you can click on the object you wish to move and toggle to the Move Gizmo. Click on the axis that you wish to move the object along and enter the distance you wish to move the object with your keyboard and press Enter.

Subcommands will allow you to define a base point and a destination point for moving the object along the selected axis as well as allowing you to copy the object instead of moving the object.

3D Rotate

Similar to the 3D Move command, the 3D Rotate command will load the Rotate Gizmo (Image 16.2). This Gizmo allows you to define an axis to rotate an object about and to define the rotation angle.

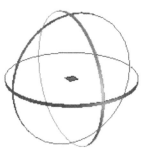

You can enter the 3D Rotate command by loading the Rotate Gizmo, by using the keyboard command 3DRO, or by clicking the 3D Rotate command in the Modeling toolbar.

If you enter the command using the Modeling toolbar or the keyboard command, the Command Line will ask you to specify which object(s) you wish to rotate. After specifying the objects, the Command Line will next ask you to specify the base point for the center of your rotation axis. Once you have clicked on screen to define the base point, the Rotate Gizmo will load at that point.

As with the Move Gizmo, the Rotate Gizmo can be repositioned by clicking on the snap point at the center of the Gizmo and dragging it around the screen with your mouse. The center of the Gizmo will become the center point of the rotation axis.

With the Rotate Gizmo loaded, click on the Gizmo to define the axis that you wish to rotate about. Finally, define how far you wish to rotate the object by either clicking on screen or defining the degree angle in the Command Line.

Similar to the two-dimensional Rotate command, subcommands within the 3D Rotate command will allow you to make a copy of the object being rotated and to use a reference angle to define the degrees of rotation.

Scale

The final Gizmo available is the Scale Gizmo (Image 16.3). The Scale Gizmo allows you to make an object larger or smaller based on a scale factor. Scale factors greater than one will cause the object to grow in size. Scale factors smaller than one (i.e. .75) will cause the object to shrink in size. You also have the ability to click on one of the ends of the Gizmo and drag your cursor to increase and decrease the size of the object.

Similar to the Move and Rotate Gizmos, prior to defining the scale factor you can choose to create a copy of the original object, or to use a reference for defining the scale factor.

Rotate 3D

The Rotate 3D command allows you to rotate objects around an axis defined by your cursor without the use of the Rotate Gizmo. When using Rotate 3D, it is important to ensure that the Orthogonal or Polar mode is turned on to ensure that you are rotating about a desired plane.

With Rotate 3D, you select the objects you wish to rotate, select the base point and define the axis to rotate around by clicking on the base point and then dragging your cursor along the rotation plan and clicking in space. You can also define a rotation axis using OSNAPS included on objects and geometry.

The Rotate 3D and 3D Rotate commands perform the same functions. For many users, the 3D Rotate command can be less confusing as it allows you to see the axis you are going to rotate around prior to completing the command; however, the alternate Rotate 3D command requires less rendering and processing power of your computer.

3D Mirror (3DMI)

The 3D Mirror command works similarly to the two-dimensional Mirror command, but allows you to define a plane other than the X-Y plane to mirror an object around.

Enter the command by typing the shortcut into the Command Line and pressing Enter. The 3D Mirror command is also available within the Modify panel on the Home tab of the Ribbon in both the 3D Modeling and 3D Basics workspaces.

After beginning the command, select the objects you wish to mirror by clicking or using a selection window and then press Enter to indicate that you have completed your selection. Next, you will need to define which plane of the UCS you wish to mirror the object about. You can use the default of 3 Points to click 3 points on your screen, or use the other subcommands to define a mirror plane along the UCS.

After you have defined the mirror plane, you will need to define a base point for the Mirror command. The base point locates the mirror plane at a specified point on the screen. Finally, the Command Line will ask you whether or not you wish to delete the source object. Select the appropriate option and press Enter to complete the command.

3D Align (3DAL)

The 3D Align command allows you to select points on an object and to align those points with points selected on another object. It is helpful to select a minimum of three points on each object for alignment.

The 3D Align command is available on the Modeling toolbar as well as within the Modify panel on the Home tab of the Ribbon in both the 3D Modeling and 3D Basics workspaces. In the 3D Basics workspace, the tool is located in a drop-down menu under the 3D Mirror tool.

After entering the command, the Command Line will ask you to select objects. Select the objects that you wish to move to a new location and press Enter.

In the 2D Align command (AL), you are asked to select the first source point followed by its destination point and so forth. In 3D Align, you first select all of your source points and then specify their destination points. After selecting the third base point, the Command Line will ask you for the first destination point. Select the point where you wish the first source point selected to land. Follow in order choosing the destination points for the second and third source points.

If the objects are not the same size, the Command Line will ask you if you wish to scale the original object so that the base points all align. Base points that do not touch will be aligned to the same plane.

3D Array

Similar to the Array command in two-dimensional drafting, the 3D Array command allows you to create an object that repeats at even intervals along a defined path. The difference between Array and 3D Array is that this command introduces the Z axis to allow you to make a cubicle array.

The Polar Array option is also available and works identically to the Polar Array option in the Array command with the exception that you can define the center of your Polar Array along any axis.

17

SOLID EDITING

To this point in the text, we have discussed how to create 3D solid objects, and how to manipulate those objects. This chapter will cover tools that allow you to change the geometry contained within a previously created 3D Object.

While I am a huge advocate of using keyboard shortcuts whenever possible to save drafting time, the keyboard shortcuts for Solid Editing tools can be cumbersome and difficult. The tools discussed in this chapter are located within the Edit panel on the Home tab of the Ribbon in the 3D Basics workspace. In the 3D Modeling workspace, they are located both in the Solid Editing panel on the Home tab of the Ribbon and in the Boolean and Solid Editing panels on the Solid tab of the Ribbon (Image 17.1).

Many of these tools can also be found on the Solid Editing toolbar, which can be docked on your screen. To access the toolbar, navigate to the Menu Bar, select Tools, hover over Toolbars and then hover over AutoCAD. Click on "Solid Editing" from the list of toolbars to load the Solid Editing toolbar to your screen.

Boolean Tools

When performing an internet or database search, Boolean Operators are simple words that help to refine the results of the search. These words include "And," "Or," "Not" and "And Not." In drafting, Boolean tools perform a similar function of creating new objects by combining multiple objects and including all or part of the geometry of the original objects. AutoCAD includes Union, Subtract and Intersect as Boolean Tools for drafting.

Union (UNI)

The Union command combines separate three-dimensional objects into a single three-dimensional object. Overlapping objects will be created so that the overlapping areas are combined. Objects that do not overlap can be combined into a single object using the Union command; however, AutoCAD will generate a warning message informing you that you are combining two non-intersecting objects. You can choose to turn this warning message off for future commands if desired.

To combine objects, enter the Union command, select all objects that you wish to combine and press Enter to complete the command. Objects that are combined using the Union command will be placed on the layer of the first object selected within the command.

Subtract (SUB)

The Subtract command removes the geometry of one object from an object that it intersects with. Subtracting a cylinder from a cube will create a hole in the cube (Image 17.2). Objects must intersect at least partially or the Subtract command will fail and the Command Line will generate an error message.

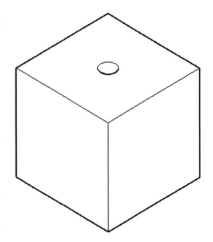

Enter the Subtract command, select the object you wish to subtract from and press Enter, then select the object you wish to subtract and press Enter. (In Image 17.2, you would select the cube first and the cylinder second.)

You may subtract one object from multiple objects in the same command; however, at the completion of the Subtract command, all objects that the subtraction was removed from will be combined into a single object, whether or not they have intersecting geometry.

Intersect

The Intersect command is essentially the opposite of the Subtract command. It will create a three-dimensional object out of the geometry of two intersecting objects. Enter the Intersect command, select the intersecting objects and press Enter. The intersecting geometry will create a new three-dimensional object and the remainder of the objects will be erased.

Slice (SL)

The Slice command allows you to cut an object along a specified plane and choose to keep one or both sides of the object. It can be helpful if you think of the Slice command in conjunction with cutting an object with a saw.

Enter the command into the Command Line and press Enter. You can also use the Slice tool from the Ribbon in both the 3D Basics and 3D Modeling workspaces. The Slice command is not included in the Modeling or Solid Editing toolbars.

After beginning the Slice command, the Command Line will ask you to select the object or objects that you wish to slice. Click on the objects you wish to slice or use a selection window to select objects and press Enter.

Next the Command Line will ask you to define the point that you wish to specify as the starting point of your slicing plane. It is often helpful before doing this to use the subcommands to define the plane you wish to cut along first. Typing XY and pressing Enter will slice an object along the X-Y axis within your drawing screen. Using the Three Point subcommand by typing "3" and pressing Enter will allow you to select three points on an existing object to use for your cutting plane.

Once you have defined the plane you wish to cut along, you will need to select the point at which you wish to make your cut. AutoCAD calls this the starting point of your slicing plane. I find it helpful to think of it as the mark on your board that you would cut with a saw. If you did not previously define the plane on which you wish to make your cut, you will have to define it at this point. To define the plane after selecting the starting point, pull your cursor to one side along the plane you wish to cut and left-click.

Finally, the Command Line will ask you to specify a point on the desired side. This prompt is asking you which side of the object you wish to keep. The default is "Both" so pressing Enter will keep both sides of the object. If you only wish to keep one side of the object, click within the drawing window on the side of the object you wish to keep.

Interfere

The Interfere command allows you to view intersecting geometry as well as to create an intersection object without erasing the original geometry.

When there are two objects that may have intersecting geometry, enter the Interfere command by typing the command INTERFERE into the Command Line and pressing Enter, or by clicking on the Interfere tool in the Ribbon. The Interfere tool is not included in the Solid Editing or Modeling toolbars.

After beginning the command, choose the first object or set of objects and press Enter. Next choose the second object or set of objects and press Enter. AutoCAD will look for objects from the first selection that interfere with objects included in the second selection.

After selecting the second set of objects, and if the objects intersect one another, AutoCAD will generate the Interference Checking dialog box (Image 17.3). Within this window, you can scroll through objects with interfering geometry by clicking the "Previous" and "Next" buttons. As you do so, the intersecting geometry will be highlighted in your drawing window. There are also buttons that allow you to close the window and enter the Zoom, Pan and Orbit commands. If the two sets of objects do not intersect each other, the Command Line will state "Objects do not interfere" and the Interference Checking dialog box will not load.

A Interference Checking   ✕

Comparing 1 object against 1 object.

Interfering objects   Highlight

First set: 1   Previous

Second set: 1   Next

Interfering pairs found: 1
                                             ☑ Zoom to pair

☑ Delete interference objects created on Close

                                        Close   Help

When closing the Interference Checking dialog box, you have the option to delete or keep the interference object. If you choose to delete the interference object, the geometry will return to what it was prior to entering the command. Unchecking the box will create an intersection object without deleting the original geometry.

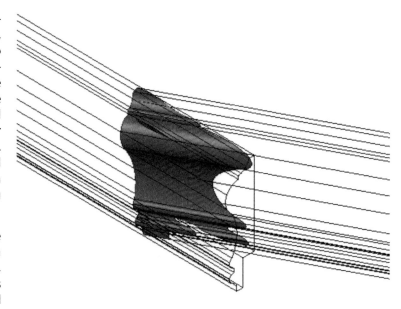

Keeping the interference objects created can often be useful. For example, when drafting moldings that require compound angles, creating an interference object allows you to have a plane to cut (slice) the molding along to accurately draft the angle required (Image 17.4).

Imprint

The Imprint command allows you to incorporate 2D Geometry as part of a 3D solid by imprinting the geometry onto a face of the 3D solid. The imprinted 2D Geometry will create a new face on the 3D Object that can be manipulated independently of other faces on the object using the Face Editing commands described below.

The 2D geometry and the 3D solid must be created prior to using the Imprint command. While text cannot be imprinted on a 3D solid, creating simple 2D geometry can allow you to imprint labels onto hardware, such as sizes and weight load ratings of rigging hardware.

To use the Imprint command, first place the 2D geometry within or on the face of the 3D solid you wish to imprint it upon. Enter the command and select the 3D solid you wish to imprint the geometry upon. (As you can only work with one solid at a time, you do not need to press Enter to indicate you have completed your selection.) After selecting the solid, select the geometry to imprint upon the solid. If the geometry is able to be imprinted upon the solid, the Command Line will ask you whether or not you wish to erase the geometry. Erasing the geometry will cause the original geometry to be deleted upon completion of the command instead of leaving the original geometry. If the geometry was not placed on the surface or within a 3D Object, the Command Line will give you an error message and the command will fail.

Face Editing

Face Editing commands allow you to manipulate one or multiple faces of a previously created 3D Object. When working in the 3D Modeling workspace, on the Home tab of the Ribbon, the Extrude Faces

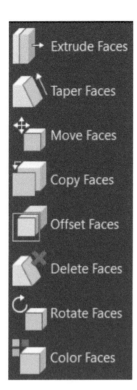

tool is contained within the Solid Editing panel. Clicking on the arrow next to this tool will load a list of available Face Editing commands (Image 17.5).

The Taper Faces, Extrude Faces and Offset Faces command are also available in the Solid tab of the Ribbon within the 3D Modeling workspace in the Solid Editing panel. In the 3D Basics workspace, they are located on the Home tab of the Ribbon within the slide out at the bottom of the Edit panel. All of the tools discussed below are also contained in the Solid Editing toolbar.

Extrude Faces

The Extrude Faces command works almost identically to the Extrude command with one exception. The Extrude command converts a 2D Shape into a 3D Object by giving it a dimension along the Z axis. The Extrude Faces command allows you to change the dimension of any face of a previously created 3D by adding or removing material to that face.

After entering the command, click all faces that you wish to change the geometry of and press Enter to indicate that you have completed your selection. (Hold Ctrl and left-click to unselect faces if you have selected a face that you no longer wish to change.)

The Command Line will now ask you to enter an extrusion height. Entering a positive number will add material to that face. Entering a negative number will remove material from that face. Once you have completed entering your extrusion height, press Enter to indicate you have completed typing your measurement. Alternately, you can choose to extrude a face along a path, such as a pre-drawn polyline or arc.

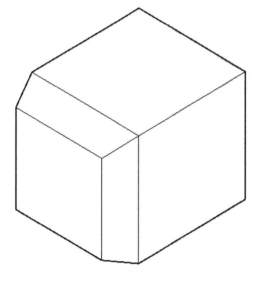

Finally, the Command Line will ask you to enter a taper angle for your face extrusion. A taper angle of 0 (which is the default angle) will add or remove material to the face chosen. Entering a taper angle other than zero will add material to that face but will create a tapered angle between the original face and the newly added geometry (Image 17.6).

With all Solid Editing commands, once you have completed the command and the geometry has successfully changed, the Command Line will enter you back into the Solid Editing toolbar. From here, using keyboard shortcuts, you can enter other Solid Editing commands. Typing the highlighted letter and pressing Enter or clicking within the Command Line will begin the new Solid Editing command selected. Pressing Escape will exit the Solid Editing toolbar and allow you access to other commands within Auto-CAD. While not as efficient as hitting the buttons, the Solid Editing commands can also be accessed by typing the command SOLIDEDIT into the Command Line.

Taper Faces

The Taper Face command allows you to add a taper into a previously drawn object by selecting the direction and the angle of the taper. Enter the command and select the face or faces you wish to taper. As with other Solid Editing commands, you can manipulate multiple faces of a single object using the command. After you have selected the faces you wish to taper, you will be asked to specify the base point and a second point along the axis of tapering. The base point will remain in its original position and the taper will be created along the plane specified by the two points.

Finally, you will be asked to define the taper angle. A positive angle will cause the taper to be created inward on the object and a negative taper will add material to the object to create the taper.

Move Faces

Using the Move Faces command, you can add or subtract geometry from the face of an object as well as moving the location of a face that exists within a 3D Object, such as changing the placement of a hole within an object.

To use the Move Face command, enter the command and choose the faces that you wish to edit. Press Enter to indicate you have completed selecting all faces that you wish to edit. The Move Faces command will now follow much of the same prompts as the Move command. You will first select a base point for your move, then select a displacement point. You can either enter a dimension for how far the face should move or use object snap points as a displacement for your face.

Copy Face

The Copy Face command allows you to create a region (a two-dimensional area) that replicates the geometry of one face of a 3D Object.

To use the Copy Face command, enter the command, select the faces you wish to copy and press Enter to indicate that you have completed your selection. The Command Line will ask you to select a base point and a displacement point. Click on the screen to select the base point, and then either click elsewhere on the screen or type a displacement distance and press Enter to define the displacement point.

AutoCAD will create an object called a region that has the exact geometry of the face you selected in the command. A region is a 2D area that has many properties of a 3D solid. The Union, Subtract and Intersect commands work with a region as they do with 3D Objects. A region also can be extruded into its own 3D Object. Exploding a region will convert it into its simplest forms (lines, arcs and circles). Using the Join command after exploding a region will convert the geometry into a closed polyline.

Offset Faces

The Offset Faces command will allow you to add or subtract geometry from the face of a previously drawn 3D Object. The Offset Face command is unique, however, in that it will allow you to change the geometry and size of a face within the object and not only on the surface of the object. For example, using the Offset Face command, you can change the diameter of a hole within an object.

While it may seem confusing at first, when using the Offset Face command, it is important to remember that using a negative number as a value for offsetting a face will remove material from the object and using a positive number for that value will add material to the object.

To use the Offset Face command to increase the diameter of a hole within an object, enter the Offset Face command, select what face you wish edit and press Enter to indicate you have completed selecting all faces that you wish to edit. Now you will enter a value for how far you wish to offset the face. Entering a negative number will remove material from the object, making the hole larger. Entering a positive number will add material to the object, making the hole smaller.

You also can use the Offset Face command to add or remove material from an exterior face of the object, but you will not be able to taper the face or extrude the face along a preexisting path as you could with the Extrude Face command.

Delete Face

The Delete Face command is used to remove a face from a 3D Object. A face cannot be deleted if deleting the face would result in a non-valid 3D solid. You cannot delete one of the six sides of a cube as doing so would not leave a defined 3D solid. However, you could use this command to delete a hole within that cube. You can also use the Delete Face command to delete chamfers and fillets drawn onto the edges of a 3D solid.

Rotate Faces

The Rotate Face command allows you to rotate the face of an object along a specified axis. In Image 17.7, the Rotate Face command could be used to rotate the slotted hole around the defined rotation access, repositioning as shown in the Hidden line.

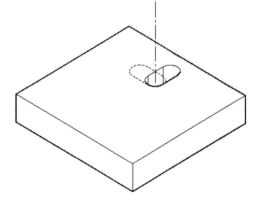

The command only works if the resulting object would produce a viable 3D Object. Enter the Rotate Face command and choose the face or faces that you wish to rotate. Similar to the Taper Face command, you will specify the rotation axis by selecting a base point and a second point along the rotation axis. You can also choose an object (such as a polyline) to define the rotation axis of or the X, Y or Z axis of your UCS. If you choose an object or the UCS to define the rotation axis, you will next need to select the origin of the rotation. This is the base point from which the rotation will occur.

Once you have defined the rotation axis and base point you will need to define the rotation angle. You can either type the angle into the Command Line or use a reference to define the rotation angle.

Color Face

The Color Face command allows you to change the color of a single face of a 3D Object. This command will allow each face of the object to have a different color, instead of the entirety of the object being a single color. This can be used to help organize a drawing, bring attention to the face of an object, or to change how that face is plotted when using color-dependent plot styles.

Enter the Color Face and select the faces that you wish to change to a different color. Note, that if you wish to change faces to multiple different colors, you will need to repeat this command for each color you wish to use. After selecting the faces you wish to edit, press Enter to indicate you have completed selecting the faces you wish to edit.

Upon completing your selection and pressing Enter, the Color Selection menu will appear on your drawing screen. Use the menu to select which color you wish to change the selected faces to and press "OK." The Color Selection menu will disappear and the faces selected will change to the color selected.

Edge Editing

Similar to the Face Editing commands, Edge Editing commands allow you to manipulate the edges of previously created 3D solids. The Fillet and Chamfer Edge commands are contained within the slide out of the Edit panel on the Home tab of the Ribbon in the 3D Basics workspace. They are also contained within the Solid Editing panel of the Solid tab of the Ribbon in the 3D Modeling workspace. All of the commands below are also contained within the Solid Editing toolbar.

Fillet Edges

The Fillet Edges command works almost identically to the Fillet command in 2D Drafting. It allows you to add a radius to selected edges of a 3D Object.

After entering the Fillet Edge command and prior to selecting an edge to apply a radius to, you will need to define what radius you would like to use. After selecting the command, the Command Line will give you a prompt to enter "R" to define the radius. If you do not complete this step, AutoCAD will default to your last used radius in this command. If you have not used this command previously, the default radius will remain 0 and AutoCAD will complete the command but you will not end with a rounded edge.

Type the radius you wish to use and press Enter to accept that radius. Next select the edges that you wish to apply the radius to. As you select the edges, AutoCAD will draw a preview of what the completed model would look like with the filleted edges. Once you have selected all edges that you wish to fillet, press Enter to indicate that you have completed your selection.

The Command Line will prompt you to "Press Enter to Accept the Fillet" or "Radius." Pressing Enter will update all geometry to the preview shown on your drawing window. Entering the Radius subcommand will allow you to change the Radius of the fillet being used on the selected edge geometry. Pressing Escape at any point prior to completing the command will abandon the command without completing the fillet on any edges selected.

It is worth noting that the Fillet (F) command typically used in two-dimensional drafting will also work to fillet the edges of a 3D Object.

Chamfer Edges

The Chamfer Edges command works nearly identically to the Fillet Edges command. The only difference is that it results in a chamfered or beveled edge at a specified distance from the original face instead of the rounded edge the Fillet Edge command provides.

After selecting the Chamfer Edge command, you will need to define the chamfer distance in the Command Line prior to selecting the edges you will chamfer. If you skip this step, AutoCAD will default to the most recently used chamfer distance. If the command has not been previously used, the default chamfer distance will remain 0 and AutoCAD will complete the command with a chamfer distance of 0 and no chamfer will be rendered.

After entering the Chamfer Edge command, the Command Line will ask you to provide the chamfer distance. You will need to provide two distances (one for each face of the edge selected). Enter the value for distance 1 and press Enter and then enter the value for distance 2 and press Enter. Now select all edges you wish to chamfer. AutoCAD will preview the chamfered edges as you make your selections. Once you have completed selecting all edges you wish to chamfer, press Enter to indicate that you have completed your selection.

AutoCAD will now ask you to press Enter to accept the chamfer or to enter the Distance subcommand to change the chamfer distances for the edges selected. Pressing Escape at any time prior to completing the Chamfer Edges command will abandon the command and delete all previewed geometry.

Copy Edges

The Copy Edge command works similarly to the Copy Face command by copying the edge of a 3D solid into a planar object. Edges that have had a chamfer or a radius applied to them have technically become an additional face of the 3D Object, and the Copy Face command must be used for these surfaces. The Copy Edge command will create lines, arcs, circles and splines based on the geometry of the edge being copied.

This new geometry can be combined into polylines and shapes using the Join command. Doing this allows you to create a two-dimensional geometry that replicates the geometry of one face of a 3D solid.

Color Edges

The Color Edge command works identically to the Color Face command. You can change the color of any edge of a 3D Object in the same way you can change the colors of faces of the object. You must reexecute the command for each color you wish to use. As with the Copy Edges command, edges that have been filleted or chamfered have become an additional face of the 3D Object and the Color Face command must be used to color these surfaces. As with the Color Faces command, changing the color of one edge of a 3D solid can bring attention to that edge and can change the way that edge prints when using color-dependent plot styles.

Clean and Check Solids

The Clean Solids command removes redundant faces, edges and vertices, while the Check Solids command ensures that you have completed a viable 3D solid in your drafting process.

Separate Solids

There are several times where you will find that you have created multiple 3D Objects from a single 3D Object. This can occur from slicing a single object on multiple planes creating separate portions of the original object, from using the Union command on non-tangential objects, or numerous other ways. The Separate Solids command will divide each non-tangential object into a standalone 3D solid.

Enter the command and click on one section of the object that you wish to separate. AutoCAD will separate each portion of the original object into its own solid. The portion of the original object you clicked on will retain the original layer properties. All other portions of the object will inherit the layer properties of your current drawing layer. Upon clicking on the object, AutoCAD will complete the command and the Command Line will reenter the menu for the Solid Editing toolbar. You can use keyboard shortcuts to reenter the Separate Solids command to repeat the command for other objects or to enter other commands within the Solid Editing toolbar. Pressing the Escape button will exit the Solid Editing toolbar and return you to the main AutoCAD window where other commands can be executed.

Shell

The final Solid Editing command discussed is the Shell command. This command allows you to create a hollowed out shape from a previously drawn 3D Object with walls of a specified dimension. While material can be removed from simple solids using the Subtract command, the Shell command can be used to hollow out more complicated solids, such as those created with the Loft command.

Enter the command by selecting the icon and then click on screen to select the object that you wish to shell. The Command Line will next ask you to select any faces you wish to remove. Any faces selected at this point will be rendered as an open side of the solid upon completion of the command. Press Enter to indicate you have completed selecting the faces to delete. You may press Enter without choosing a face if you do not wish to have an open side of your solid or you may select one or multiple sides of the solid.

After completing your selection of faces to delete and pressing Enter the Command Line will ask you to define the shell offset distance. This will allow you to define the thickness of the walls of your shelled object. Enter your offset distance in inches (or the unit of measurement you are using) and press Enter. Your solid will now be rendered with a hollow core and any surfaces chosen to be deleted during the command will now have only the wall thickness of the solid on that surface.

18

PLATING 3D MODELS

Drafting objects in 3D in Model Space allows the draftsperson to see objects more clearly and how they interact with one another. For an experienced draftsperson, 3D modeling will actually save time in drafting over a 2D drafting style. It can allow for more accurate and precise drafting and for clearer conversations to be had among collaborators during the drafting phase. However, as a TD I have never handed my laptop to a shop crew and asked them to go build a set. Instead, a plate of 2D drafting representing the 3D object or assembly is handed off to the shop crew for the build. Similarly, designers hand off paper or PDF packets to crew leads for budgeting and engineering.

This chapter will discuss how to take a 3D model from Model Space and create a 2D drafting in Paper Space. Once that drafting is created, the Annotation tools used and discussed with 2D drafting can be used to finish the drafting plate.

While it has been discussed throughout the book, it is worth repeating here. AutoCAD for Mac is a different program than AutoCAD. AutoCAD is best used on a 64-Bit PC machine. The last portion of this chapter will discuss the View Base command and the options available therein. The View Base command is the fastest method of laying out 3D models into Paper Space. This command allows the user to create a drafting plate from a 3D model in the matter of a few minutes, significantly reducing drafting time from any other method available. This command, however, is only available when using AutoCAD on a 64-Bit Windows Platform.

Plating Using Viewports

Chapter 11 of this text discusses how to use Viewports to plot 2D drafting. It is possible to use the same method to plot 3D models, and then within the Viewport to select which view you wish to see (Top, Right, Front, etc.) displayed in the Viewport. This can be the most familiar way of creating drafting plates for those who do not use 3D modeling very often.

Step 1: Create Viewports

Begin by selecting a Layout tab to use for your drafting plate. Insert one or multiple Viewports following the same steps used in 2D drafting. As a reminder, MV is the keyboard command for creating a Model View. It is helpful to set your Model View Windows to be on a "Do Not

Print" layer to prevent from seeing the borders of the window when you print your drafting plate.

Step 2: Select a view direction

Activate the Viewport by double-clicking inside of it. Using either the View button in the top left of the Viewport window or any other view tool, select the view from which you wish to display the objects. Note that when you change your view angle, AutoCAD will zoom to the extents of all objects displayed in Model Space.

Step 3: Zoom and Pan to the objects you wish to display within the Viewport

Step 4: Freeze layers to display only the objects you wish to show. With your cursor in an activated Viewport, using the "Freeze in Viewport" tool will freeze layers only within the activated Viewport, allowing them to be visible in Model Space and within other Viewports.

Step 5: Ensure views are in orthographic layout

Once you have selected the views to use in each Viewport, you will need to ensure that views of a single object are oriented in an orthographic layout. The Move command can be used to move a Viewport and the content contained within that Viewport to new locations on the screen. Geometry within each of the Viewports can be used as snapping and reference points for aligning the Viewports, even if the Viewport is not activated. You can also utilize construction geometry on the layout to help with alignment.

Step 6: Choose a Visual Style for the printed page

Click on the Viewport with which you are working (do not double click inside the Viewport). With the outline of the Viewport highlighted, navigate to the Properties Manager. (The keyboard shortcut CH will load your Properties Manager if it is not currently loaded.) In the Properties Manager navigate to the "Shade Plot" selection near the bottom of the panel. The default for the Shade Plot variable is "As Displayed." To change this, click on the words "As Displayed" and a drop-down menu will appear allowing you to change this variable (Image 18.1).

While the "As Displayed" variable works for smaller files, when working in a larger drawing it saves considerable processing power to leave your Viewports in a 2D wireframe view and to change the Shade Plot variable in your Properties Manager. This will prevent your computer from needing to render shaded, hidden, grayscale or other views in each Viewport, while allowing the finished drafting plate to print with the selected plot shading.

A Note about Hidden Lines

Even when selecting the Hidden Line plot style from the Shade Plot command, AutoCAD will hide your "hidden objects" instead of making them hidden lines without making a couple of adjustments to the standard AutoCAD setup. To change this default, navigate to the Visual Styles Manger (Image 18.2) by typing the keyboard shortcut VIS into the Command Line and pressing Enter. At the top of the Visual Style Manager, select the image for the Hidden Visual Style. In the bottom half of the manager window scroll to the section labeled "Occluded Edges." Change the variable for "Show" from no to yes. Next select the line type that you wish to use for your hidden lines (usually a dashed or medium dashed line). When you have completed these changes, exit the Visual Styles Manager by clicking the small x at the top left corner of the window. After making these changes, any Viewports that are shaded for the Hidden Visual Style will now display occluded objects as dashed or hidden lines. This will remain true for all future drawings

until you change it again in the Visual Styles Manager. It can also be accomplished using the same methods for other visual styles.

While this is a quick fix to show hidden lines on the printed page, it does come with some downsides. Changing the Visual Styles Manager so that occluded edges are shown in the Layout tab will also cause them to appear in Model Space, which isn't always desired. The Visual Style Manager also does not offer all line types for use in showing occluded edges, meaning that you are required to use a dashed line instead of a hidden line to show occluded edges.

Section

The command SECTION (SEC) allows you to specify three points of a cutting plane and creates a drawing of the boundaries of the objects being sectioned. The Section command will work on 3D objects, but will not work on blocks. To draw a section of items included in a block, the block will first need to be exploded into its basic 3D object parts prior to using the Section command.

Enter the Section command, select the objects you wish to include in your section drawing and press Enter to indicate that you have completed your selection. The Command Line will next ask you to select the points on the cutting plane. Click on three points that define your cutting plane. There must be one point each on the X, Y and Z axis. After specifying the cutting plane, AutoCAD will create regions from the 3D solids that make the section view along the cutting plane. These regions are left on the original cutting plane. The section can be placed on a separate layer and viewed through a Viewport, set to a specific scale and annotated.

As the Section command only shows the boundaries of the sectioned objects, appropriate hatching would need to be added.

While the Section tool can be used to plate section views of objects, it is best used as a quick visual tool in Model Space. Using the section tool for plating drawings can be a laborious process, and there are other commands that are better at doing this.

Section Plane

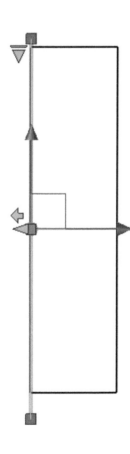

The Section Plane tool allows you to define a cutting plane and then creates a section view, complete with hatching, of all objects that cross through that cutting plane. The Section Plane tool is located on the Home tab of the Ribbon within the 3D Modeling workspace. You can also enter the command using the keyboard command SECTIONPLANE.

After entering the Section Plane command, the Command Line will prompt you to "Select face or any point to locate section line." Clicking on the face of a 3D solid will place the Section Plane on the face selected. Alternately, clicking in space will start a drawing of a Section Plane. Drag your cursor away from the starting point of the Section Plane and click on the screen to define the end point of the Section Plane. After defining the end point, a Section Plane will appear on your screen, and half of the geometry that crosses through that plane will disappear from your screen (Image 18.3).

Clicking on the drawing of the Section Plane will load the Move Gizmo onto the Section Plane, as well as object grips and two small arrows. The Move Gizmo can be used to move the location of the Section Plane. Right-clicking on the Move Gizmo will load the shortcut menu where you can toggle to the Rotate and Scale Gizmos to reposition the Section Plane. The small arrow at the top of the Section Plane allows you to change the behavior of the Section Plane. The small arrow near the center of the Section Plane allows you to change the direction of view about the Section Plane (showing the left side instead of the right). Additionally, when you click on the Section Plane, the Ribbon will load the Section Plane tools (Image 18.4).

Clicking on the Live Section tool to the left of the Ribbon will toggle the Live Section on and off. Turning the Live Section off will cause the geometry that was hidden at the creation of the Section Plane to reappear. Clicking on the diagonal arrow at the bottom of the Live Section panel will load the Section Settings dialog box (Image 18.5). The Section Settings dialog box is also accessible using the keyboard command SECTIONPLANE-SETTINGS. From this dialog box, you can define the behavior of 2D and 3D sections, as well as that of the Live Section tool. With the Live Section button selected, scrolling to the bottom of the dialog box will allow you to control the behavior of the cutaway geometry, including showing it in a different color.

The Modify panel allows you to change the behavior of the Section Plane (duplicating the drop-down arrow located at the top of the Section Plane) as well as to add a jog to the Section Plane and to rotate the Section Plane 90 degrees. The Adjust panel allows you to adjust the thickness of a slice plane. To the right of the Ribbon is the Generate Section Block tool. This tool allows you to create a block that contains either a 2D or 3D section of the cut geometry. A 2D section will be a flat planar surface that includes the boundaries of the sectioned geometry as well as hatching. A 3D section will create a 3D model of the sectioned geometry. This model is converted into a block that includes 3D solids and can be manipulated separately from the original model.

After entering the Create Section Block tool, you will be asked to select the Section Plane you wish to use to create the block. After selecting

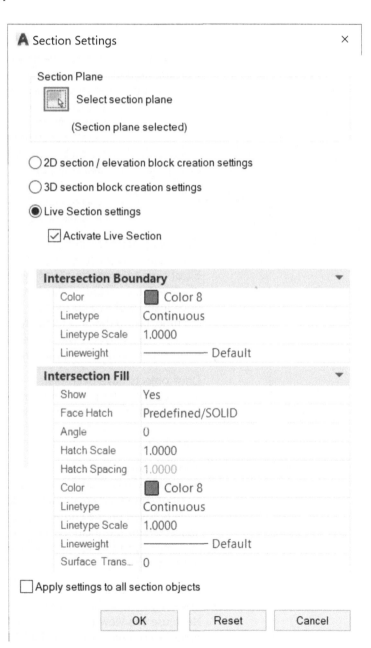

the Section Plane, you will need to specify the location on the screen to draw the new section as well as the scale and rotation of the new block.

Section Planes can be placed on a do not print layer if you wish for them to not appear on the printed page. Additionally, section blocks will remain in the drawing once they have been created even if the Section Plane used to create them is deleted from the drawing. Once a section has been created, it can be placed within a Viewport and set to a specific scale for plotting.

Drawing Detail Views

Detail views provide enhanced views and more information for specific parts included in a drafting plate. Detail views should be drawn on the same drafting plate of the drawing they are referencing (Image 18.6). To use a Viewport to create a detail view, first place a circle or rectangular indicator around the area you are going to detail. Then within a second Viewport and at a larger scale place the detail view. Create the Viewport in the same shape as the detail indicator. If you use a circular indicator, draw a circle on the page and then use the MV command and the Object subcommand to turn the circle into a Viewport. Set the Viewport to show the area being detailed and set the detail view to a specified scale. Label the detail indicator with a letter and label the detail view with the corresponding letter and the scale of the detail view.

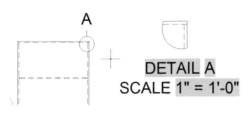

Using Viewports to plate 3D models can feel familiar and intuitive as it replicates the practices used in 2D drafting. While it may take a little bit of time to organize a drafting plate so that the correct views are displayed in an orthographic layout, the ability to draft an object only once instead of having to draw each individual view will save drafting time. Taking the time to create a template drawing with commonly used Viewport layouts within the Paper Space Layout tabs will help to prevent the need for continued recreation of drafting plates.

Once objects have been plated, the Annotation and Dimension tools are used to finish the drafting plate. These tools are used in an identical manner as they are with 2D drafting.

Flatshot

Another method for plating 3D objects when you don't have access to the View Base command is to use the command FLATSHOT. The Flatshot command creates a two-dimensional representation of all 3D objects based on the current view. All objects displayed on the Model Space screen are included in this representation. With the Flatshot command, you can also choose to show the obscured lines within the drawing as Hidden lines.

Use the Hide Objects or Isolate Objects command to ensure only the objects you wish to include are displayed on your drawing screen. Next, use the View tools to navigate to the view you wish to display. Type the command FLATSHOT into the Command Line and press Enter.

The Flatshot dialog box will display on your screen (Image 18.7).

Within the Flatshot dialog box, select what you want to happen to the Flatshot when it is created. It is typical to leave this as the default and have the Flatshot inserted as a new block into the current Model Space drawing; however, you may also choose to export it to a new drawing file in a location you specify.

Next select the line color and line type for the foreground lines, select whether or not you wish to show obscured and hidden lines, and whether or not to show tangential lines. To follow theatrical drafting standards, select to show the obscured lines as a hidden line type, and select to include tangential lines.

Once you have completed your selections in the Flatshot Creation dialog box, click the "Create" button and AutoCAD will create the Flatshot. Once the Flatshot is created, the Command Line will prompt you to select an insertion point. Click within the drawing window to define this point. The Command Line then will ask you to define the scale for the drawing on the X axis. Typically the scale is 1:1, which is the default so you can press Enter. Next the Command Line will prompt you to define the scale for the drawing on the Y axis. Once again, this is typically 1:1 (the default) so press Enter again. Finally, the Command Line will ask you to define the rotation angle. Typically this is 0, which is the default, so you can press Enter one more time to complete the command. Keeping the scale of the Flatshot at 1:1 keeps the geometry at the original size, allowing you to set it to scale within a Viewport and dimension the geometry correctly.

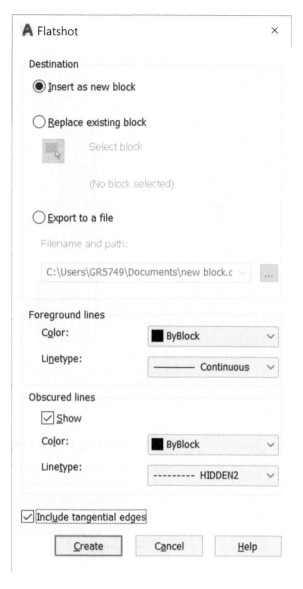

View Base

Perhaps the fastest method of plating a drafting from a 3D AutoCAD model is to use the View Base command. The View Base command creates a base view in a Layout tab (Top, Front, etc.) defined by the user from solids and surfaces that exist within Model Space. Projected views, including orthographic and isometric views, sections and detail views can then be created from the base view. If no 3D objects exist within your Model Space tab, the "Select File" dialog box is opened where you can select objects from an AutoDesk Inventor File.

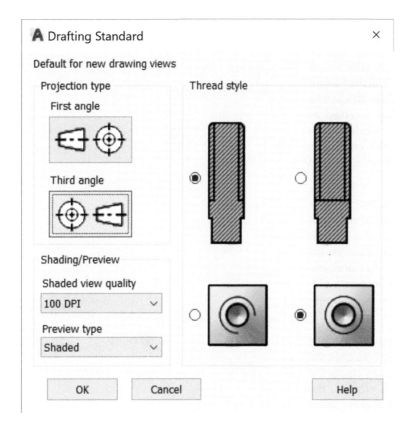

The View Base command is located on the extreme right end of the Home tab of the Ribbon in both the 2D Drafting and Annotation and the 3D Modeling workspaces. You can also use the command VIEWBASE to begin the command. The command VIEWEDIT allows you to make changes to drawing views created using the View Base command.

Clicking on the diagonal arrow at the bottom right corner of the View Base panel on the Ribbon will load the Drafting Standards dialog box (Image 18.8). This dialog box allows you to define the behavior of views created with the View Base command.

Creating a Base View

The default in the AutoCAD program is to draw the base view of your model on whichever Layout tab was most recently selected. While it is possible to change which Layout tab to draw the base view on during the view creation process, you can also click on the Layout tab you wish to use prior to returning to Model Space to begin the View Base command.

After entering the command, the Command Line will prompt you to "Select Objects" or to use the "Entire Model." Using the entire model will include all 3D objects in your base view. The default is to use the entire model, so pressing Enter before selecting objects will create a base view of all 3D objects visible in Model Space. If you wish to use only some objects within Model Space, click on the objects you wish to include or use a selection window to choose which objects to include and press Enter to indicate you have completed your selection.

Next, the Command Line will prompt you to define which Layout tab to use when creating the base view from your Model Space objects. This will default to the most recently used Layout tab. Press Enter to accept the default and move to the next step of the process. If you wish to change the Layout tab being used, type the name of the Layout tab in the Command Line exactly as it appears in the Layout tab and press Enter.

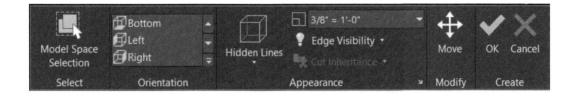

Once the Layout tab has been selected, AutoCAD will place you in that Layout tab and open the Drawing View Creation tab on the Ribbon. (Image 18.9) Clicking within the Layout page will "drop" your base view to the location you clicked on. The Command Line will then provide a list of options for viewing the base view, including which orientation to use (top, front, side, etc.) what visual style to use (hidden lines, grayscale, etc.) and what scale to use. These options are duplicated in the Ribbon.

Clicking on the "Model Space Selection" button on the left of the Drawing View Creation tab of the Ribbon will return you to Model Space where you can add or remove objects from the base view. The Orientation tab allows you to select which orientation to use for your base view. The Appearance panel allows you to choose which visual line type to use, as well as what scale to use for the drawing view. The Move function will allow you to move the location of the base view. The OK button will complete the base view and the Cancel button will abandon the command. Pressing the Escape button at any time prior to the completion of the drawing view creation will abandon the command and return you to Model Space.

After making the appropriate selections for your base view, you can either click the "OK" button in the Drawing View Creation tab of the Ribbon or press Enter to indicate that the base view has been completed. AutoCAD will next put you into the projected view creation mode.

Creating Projected Views

After placing your base view in the Layout tab, use your cursor to drag your mouse to the side, top, bottom or diagonally and left-click in space to create projected views. AutoCAD will draw a projected view of the objects from the base view in the correct orientation. These projected views will be locked in an orthographic layout. If you move a front view of an object up or down, the projected side view will also move up or down on the page to remain in orthographic alignment.

AutoCAD will allow you to make, however, many projected views you wish by dragging your cursor in the direction of the projected view and clicking in space. Once you have "dropped" the projected views you wish to draw, press Enter to exit the Drawing Creation tool.

Drawing View Editor

To edit a drawing previously created using the View Base command, click on the drawing in the Layout tab. The Ribbon will load the Drawing View tab (Image 18.10). Selecting the Edit button from this tab will

return you to the Drawing View Editor tab of the Ribbon where you can change any of the options you chose in the drawing view creation process. You also will have the option to add projected views in the Drawing View tab of the Ribbon within the Create View panel.

Creating Section Views

To create a section view, click on a base or projected view from a drawing previously created using the View Base tools. This will load the Drawing View tab in the Ribbon. Next, click on the "Section" button in the Create View panel of the Ribbon. Clicking on the arrow below the section view button will load a list of section types. Clicking on the Section panel button will default to using a full section view the first time it is used. If you change and use a different section type, the default will change to the most recently used type of section view until it is changed again by the user. After choosing what type of section to use, the Section View Creation tab will load in the Ribbon (Image 18.11).

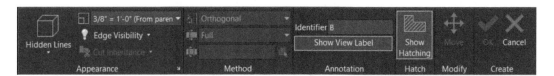

Along with the Section View Creation tab being displayed in the Ribbon, AutoCAD will also put a Cutting Plane tool connected to the cross hairs of your cursor. Define the cutting plane by clicking at least two points that intersect the object you are drawing a section from. Press Enter to indicate that you have completed drawing your cutting plane. Next drag your cursor and click in space to define where to draw the section view. Notice that the arrows of the viewing direction automatically change depending on where the section view is placed.

Next, use the tools in the Section View Creation panel to define the scale of the section, the visual line styles, the identifier or label of the section view, whether or not to show hatching and to change section styles (from full to half, etc.). Click the OK button or press Enter to complete the section view. AutoCAD will draw the section view, with appropriate hatching and create a label for the section view.

Section View Style Manager

At the bottom of the View panel on the Home tab of the Ribbon is an arrow pointing straight down. Clicking on this arrow will load a slide out that defines the styles being used for Section and Detail Views (Image 18.12). Clicking on the top left button within this slide out will load the Section View Style Manager where you can modify or create Section View Styles.

Click on the "Modify" button to modify the existing style or the "New" button to create a new Section View Style. Choosing the "New" button will allow you to define a Section View Style to use as a starting point for creating the new style.

The Section View Style Modification dialog box (Image 18.13) allows you to define the behavior of indicators, cutting planes, labels and hatching included in a Section drawing.

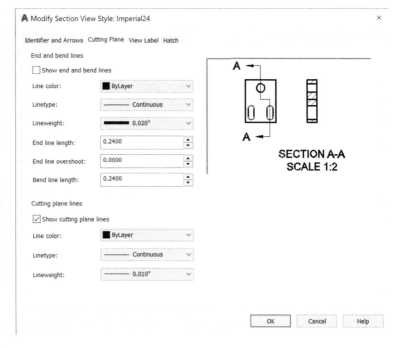

Creating Detail Views

Creating detail views using the View Base tools follows a similar pattern to drawing section views. To create a detail view, click on a drawing previously created using the View Base tools. The Drawing View tab will once again load in the Ribbon. From here select the Detail button located in the Create View panel of the Ribbon. This will load the Detail View Creation tab in the Ribbon (Image 18.14).

Click to select the center point of the area you wish to detail and then drag your cursor away from the center to define the outer edge of the area you wish to detail. Next click on screen to define the placement of the detail view. Use the options in the Detail View Creation tab to change the style of the detail from circular to rectangular, to change the scale of the detail view, to change the label and to change the visual appearance of the edge of the model. Click on the "OK" button or press Enter to indicate that you have completed your selections. AutoCAD will draw the detail view in the defined location and add appropriate labeling.

Detail View Style Manager

Similar to the Section View Style Manager, the Detail View Style Manager (Image 18.15) can be loaded using the button on the slide out of the View panel on the Home tab of the Ribbon. It is the button directly below the Section View Style Manager. The Detail View Style Manager allows you to define the behavior of the detail identifier, the boundary and the view label.

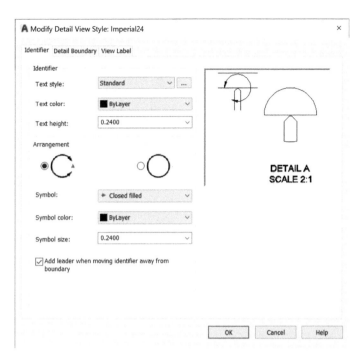

Dimensions and Annotations

Once you have placed the views of your 3D model in Paper Space, you can use the Annotation tools to add dimensions and notes. These follow the same process used in two-dimensional drafting.

19

CAMERA VIEWS AND ANIMATION

To this point in the text, we have focused exclusively on creating and plating drafting. In this chapter, we will discuss two methods for using AutoCAD's Model Space as a primary means of presentation for design conversation. While the plated drafting is still the most effective means of communicating the full details of a project, going through a full drafting and detailing process can be unnecessary in early stages of the design process. While sharing an AutoCAD drafting is always an option, many of those whom you are collaborating with will not have the software installed and will not be able to open your files. Creating isometric views is a good option for showing a general idea of a scenic design from an AutoCAD drawing, but it doesn't provide an actual view that scenery would be observed from as an audience member. Auto-CAD allows you to create camera views, which allow you to specify a specific angle to view a 3D AutoCAD model from. Camera tools allow you to place an image of a camera in a drawing and then to manipulate that image in much the same way you would a camera to capture an image of the 3D model.

Definitions of Camera Properties

Before beginning the process of creating a camera view in Model Space, it is helpful to first understand the definition of terms that AutoCAD uses to define the properties of the camera view.

Location:

Defines the location of the camera, or the point from which you are viewing the 3D model.

Target:

Defines the point you are viewing through the camera lens.

Lens length:

Defines the magnification properties of the camera lens. Similar to photography cameras, using a longer lens length will create a narrower Field of View.

Clipping Planes:

AutoCAD allows you to create clipping planes where you can hide, or clip, objects from the view of the camera. A front clipping plane will hide everything between the camera and the clipping plane. A back clipping plane will hide everything between the target of the camera and the clipping plane.

In the 3D Modeling workspace, the Camera panel exists within the Visualize tab of the Ribbon. It is hidden by default until it is activated by the user. To activate the Camera tools, navigate to the Visualize tab of the Ribbon, right-click anywhere within the Ribbon and hover over the Show Panels option in the right-click menu. Click on Camera and the Camera panel will load in the Ribbon. From here you can create cameras, toggle the cameras on and off and make adjustments to previously created cameras.

Creating Camera Views

It is perhaps easiest to begin the creation of a camera view by setting your 3D model to an isometric view. This allows you to see all three axis of the 3D model when placing the camera. To begin the creation of the camera view, click on the Create Camera tool in the Camera panel of the Visualize tab of the Ribbon or enter the command CAMERA (CAM) in the Command Line and press Enter.

Upon entering the Camera command, an image of a camera will be attached to the mouse cursor. Clicking in space will define the position of the camera. After defining the position of the camera, the Field

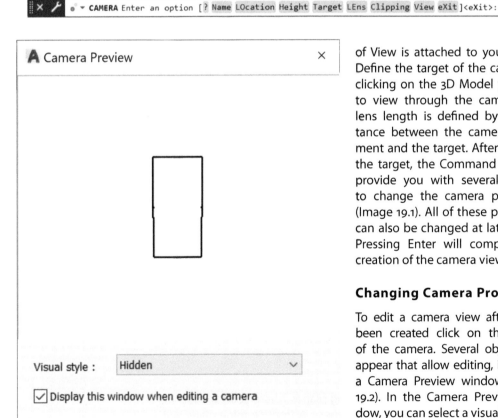

of View is attached to your cursor. Define the target of the camera by clicking on the 3D Model you wish to view through the camera. The lens length is defined by the distance between the camera placement and the target. After defining the target, the Command Line will provide you with several options to change the camera properties (Image 19.1). All of these properties can also be changed at later times. Pressing Enter will complete the creation of the camera view.

Changing Camera Properties

To edit a camera view after it has been created click on the image of the camera. Several objects will appear that allow editing, including a Camera Preview window (Image 19.2). In the Camera Preview window, you can select a visual style for that camera and see real-time adjustments being made to the camera. There is also an option to choose not to show the Camera Preview window when making adjustments to the camera.

Object Grips

Several Object Grips appear on the camera and Field of View box when you click on a previously created camera (Image 19.3). The Object Grip on the camera allows you to move the position of the camera. The Object Grip in the middle of the Field of View box allows you to move the camera closer to and further away from the target. The Object Grip at the end of the Field of View box allows you to change the target of the camera.

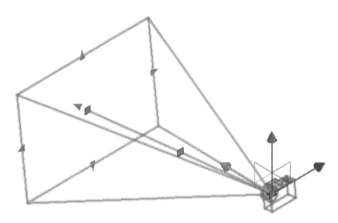

Four arrows also appear at the end of the Field of View box. Manipulating these arrows allows you to adjust the length of the camera lens, narrowing and widening the Field of View.

Move and Rotate Gizmos

When you click on a camera, the 3D Move Gizmo is attached to the camera, allowing you to change the position of the camera along the X, Y or Z axis. Right-clicking on the Gizmo allows you to toggle to the Rotate and Scale Gizmos. The Rotate Gizmo can be used to adjust the Field of View of the camera and the Scale Gizmo can be used to change the size of the camera in Model Space.

Changing Names of Camera Views

By default, AutoCAD names camera views "Camera View 1," "Camera View 2" and so forth. AutoCAD provides an option to change the name of a camera view to a user-defined name. To change the name of a camera view, navigate to the View tab of the Ribbon in the 3D Modeling workspace and click on the View Manager tool in the Named Views panel. This will load the View Manager (Image 19.4). Within the View Manager, click on the plus sign next to the word

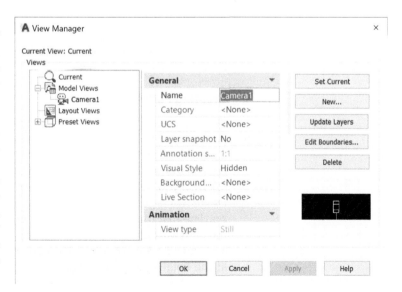

"Model Views" in the list on the left and then click on the camera that you wish to change the name of. In the middle of the toolbox, highlight the name of the camera view and type the name you wish to give to the view. Finally, click the "OK" button at the bottom of the toolbox to save your changes.

The View Manager can also be used to name and save custom views of a 3D model without using cameras, such as a specific view that can typically only be viewed through use of the Orbit command. To do this, set the model to the desired view and then use the "Current" option in the View Manager.

Plating Camera Views

Camera views can be plated using a Viewport. Instead of selecting a top, side or isometric view to display in the Viewport, hover your mouse over "Custom Model Views" and then select the name of the camera you wish to display within the Viewport.

Hiding Cameras in Model Space

Camera views can be useful tools to communicate and collaborate, but having images of cameras littering your model space can be awkward or cumbersome. To hide cameras within Model Space, but to keep the ability to use the camera views, you can toggle the images of the cameras on and off by using the Camera Display tool located under the Create Camera tool in the Ribbon. Clicking the button once will turn off the images of all cameras in the drawing. Clicking it again will turn the images back on, allowing you access to make edits to camera views.

Motion Path Animation

An Animated Motion Path allows you to create a video walk through of a 3D AutoCAD model. Within the creation of this animation, you can either affix the camera that is doing the recording to a single point or have it travel along a predefined path. Likewise, you can also have the Field of View attached to a single point while the camera moves, have the Field of View move while the camera stays stationary or have the Field of View move along a predetermined path while the camera moves along a separate path.

Creating Paths

Prior to creating a Motion Path Animation, you will need to create paths. If you wish to have the camera move, you will need to create a path to attach the camera to. If you wish to have the target of the camera move, you will likewise need to create a path for the target to follow. If you wish to have both move simultaneously, you will need to create two separate paths. The easiest way to create a path is to draw a polyline that the camera or its target can use for their paths. Note that the path will begin at the point where you started drawing the polyline and end where you finished. The path for the camera should be placed at the height you wish to view the animation from. The path for the target should likewise be placed at an appropriate height for the viewing angle of the camera.

Accessing the Motion Path Animation Toolbox

Similar to the Camera tools, the Animation tools within AutoCAD exist on the Ribbon within the 3D Modeling workplace. Also, similar to the Camera tools, the Animation tools are hidden by default within the Ribbon. To access the Animation tools within AutoCAD, set your workspace to 3D Modeling and navigate to the Visualize tab of the Ribbon. Right-click anywhere within the Ribbon, hover your cursor over the "Show Panels" button and click on the "Animation" button.

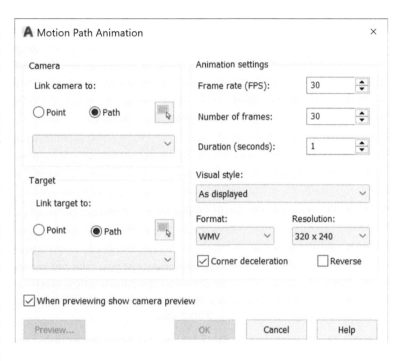

Once the Animation panel is loaded into the Ribbon, click on the "Animation Motion Path" at the left of the Animation panel to load the Motion Path Animation dialog box (Image 19.5).

Within the Motion Path Animation dialog box, you can choose to attach the camera and the target to a single point or to a path.

To attach the camera or the target to a path, click on the path selection and then click on the icon to right. Your cursor will be placed in Model Space where you can select the path to attach the camera to. If you wish to attach the camera or the path to a single point, click on the point selection icon, and then specify the point by clicking a point in Model Space.

On the right of the toolbox are options to allow you to adjust the video features, including the length of the video, the frames per second the video is shot in, how many total frames to include, which file format to save the video in, which visual style to use for the video as well as the resolution of the video. You can also use the selection boxes to choose to reverse the video path and to choose whether or not to decelerate the pace of the video as the camera goes around corners. Once you have made your selections, you can preview the video using the Preview button in the bottom left corner of the toolbox. Once you have finalized your video, clicking OK will load a File Manger window allowing you to define a save location for the video created.

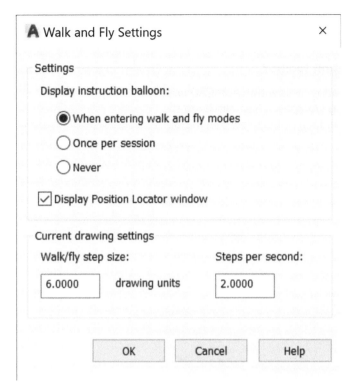

Walk and Fly

One additional tool that exists within the Animation panel is the Walk and Fly Animation tools. This Animation tool allows you to begin from a perspective view (such as a camera) and then walk or fly through a 3D model in AutoCAD. While the Walk and Fly tools perform in much the same manner, when using the Walk tool you are constrained to moving along only the X and Y axis, while you are not constrained when using the Fly tool.

To access the Walk and Fly Settings dialog box (Image 19.6), click the drop-down menu next to the Walk/Fly tool in the Animation panel of the Ribbon and click on "Walk and Fly Settings." This dialog box allows you to change the size of a step (how far you travel per step) as well as how many steps you take per second. There are also other options to allow you to customize how often to show instructions and whether or not to show a Display Position Locator window when using the Walk and Fly tools.

Once you have defined the settings for your Walk and Fly tools, you can enter the command by clicking on the button in the Animation panel in the ribbon. The same drop-down menu where the settings toolbox is located will allow you to switch between the Walk and Fly tools.

To Walk and Fly, use your arrow keys to go forward and backward, and right and left. The green cross hair on the screen is the target to which you are walking toward or away from. Drag your mouse around the screen to change the target location.

You can record a Walk or Fly session using the Record, Stop, Play and Pause buttons that are included in the Animation panel of the Ribbon. Once you have completed a recording of a Walk or Fly session, the File Manager of your computer will load, allowing you to save the video file.

20

AUTOCAD FOR PRODUCTION AND ENGINEERING

The final chapter of this text includes an eclectic arrangement of processes and commands that assist in the sharing of files during the production process, as well as assisting in the engineering of scenic components. While none of these processes and commands merits a dedicated chapter, all of them can reduce drafting time and provide tools that can be used during engineering and production.

The Design Center

The Design Center is a useful tool that allows you to share design elements within your own drawings, as well as between colleagues and consultants who have shared files with you. It allows you to import Blocks, Layouts, Visual Styles, Text Styles and much more from other drawings without the need to open those drawings.

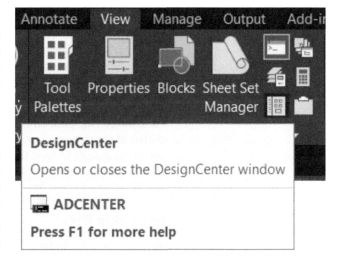

To access the Design Center, type the keyboard command DC into the Command Line and press Enter. Alternately, navigate to the View tab within the Ribbon and select the Design Center tool under the Palettes panel (Image 20.1).

On the left of the Design Center, you can choose to view AutoCAD files that are currently open on your device, or to search through your computers File Manager for files that you have access to.

Once you have selected a file, options will be given on the right side of the palette to allow you to import items from the selected file into the current file. For example, you could import a title block from a previous drawing into this drawing to prevent needing to draw that item again.

To import a block from another drawing, highlight the drawing you are importing from on the left side of the palette by clicking on the file. Next, double-click on the Blocks tool on the right side of the palette. The right side of the palette will now load all of the block definitions that exist within the file you are importing from. Select the block you

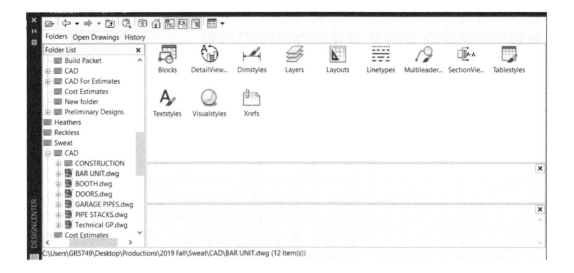

C:\Users\GR5749\Desktop\Productions\2019 Fall\Sweat\CAD\BAR UNIT.dwg (12 Item(s))

wish to insert into the new drawing by double clicking on your selection. The Insert Block menu will load, allowing you to insert that block into the new drawing. You can also drag and drop the block from one drawing to the other within the Design Center.

Use the back and forward buttons at the top of the Design Center palette to navigate through objects, items and files saved to your device. Use the same method used for importing blocks to import other items and objects into the new drawing using the Design Center.

Exporting Files

AutoCAD saves drawing files as .dwg file types. However, AutoCAD will also allow you to export your drawings as different file types to allow you to share your AutoCAD drawings with other computer-aided drafting software.

To export a File, click on the AutoCAD Menu (the big A at the top left corner of the screen), then navigate to and hover over the "Export Files" tool (Image 20.3). Choose the option for the file type you wish to export. AutoCAD will open the File Manager from your device and allow you to specify where to save the exported file.

Importing Files

Similar to exporting files, AutoCAD will allow you to import files from other file types. AutoCAD will also allow you to drag and drop several file types into your AutoCAD drawing, including PDFs and 3D SAT models.

Preparing AutoCAD Files for CNC Programming

While it is not possible to program a CNC (Computer Numerical Control) machine directly from an AutoCAD file, there are steps to follow when drafting in AutoCAD to ensure that your CNC programs can read and properly interpret your drafting.

CNC programming software typically operates from non DWG file types (such as DXF). It can be helpful to create a separate CAD file that contains only items to be cut with a CNC machine. Some programmers prefer to have a single file for each object being cut, while other programmers prefer a single file containing all objects to be programmed for a CNC machine. With the AutoCAD file ready, select "Save As" from the AutoCAD menu in the top left corner of the screen. Prior to saving the drawing, click on the arrow next to "Files of Type" in the File Manager and select the file type that is compatible with your CNC machine.

Most CNC programs and cut paths operate best when provided with closed polylines and closed circles as geometry. When performing 2D CAD functions, ensuring that you are drafting in closed polylines and shapes will ensure that your CNC program can accurately produce the objects drafted. When creating 3D models, 2D geometry will need to be created that replicates the face of the geometry being cut on the CNC machine. There are several ways to accomplish this, three of which are detailed below.

Method 1 Flatshot

1. Use the Layer and Isolate tools to display only the objects you wish to work with for the CNC file
2. Place the drawing in the appropriate view so that you can view the sides of the objects that will be cut on the CNC
3. Perform the Flatshot command to create a block with the two-dimensional geometry
4. Explode the block and run the Overkill command to clean up the geometry
5. Use the Join command to create closed shapes to follow best practices for CNC machining

6. Rotate the geometry so that it is viewed from a top view within your AutoCAD model space. (Failure to do this may cause your geometry to be displaced when you import your file into the CNC programming software.)

Method 2 Copy Faces

7. Perform a Copy Face command to create a region from the face you wish to cut with the CNC machine
8. Use the Explode command to explode the newly created region into its component parts
9. Use the Join command to combine all of the component parts into closed polylines and shapes
10. Use the 3D Rotate command to rotate the new polylines and shapes so that they are viewed from a top view within your AutoCAD model space. (Failure to complete this step may cause your objects to be displaced when you import your file into your CNC programming software.)

Method 3 Copy Edges

This follows a similar pattern as the Copy Faces method, except that you copy the edges of the solid and then use the Join command to combine those copied edges into closed shapes and polylines.

3D Printers

As opposed to CNC programs, 3D printers are specifically looking for individual objects in their programming files. Most 3D printers operate from .STL file extension types. To export a single object from an AutoCAD file to a .STL file, first select the object by clicking on the object you wish to export. Next, from the AutoCAD menu at the top left of the screen select "Export" and then select "Other Formats" from the selection window. A File Manager window will load on your screen. Select the Lithography (STL) file format and then define the name and the save location of the STL File. This will allow you to import the STL file into your 3D printer software where you can program the object accordingly.

Mass Properties

Many structural engineering calculations are based upon the geometry of an object or an assembly of objects. The Mass Properties command in AutoCAD will calculate and provide you with the value of these calculations based upon the geometry within your AutoCAD model.

Mass properties can be provided for 2D regions as well as 3D objects and assemblies. It is important when using the Mass Properties command for use in engineering that you use accurate geometry for the shapes of the objects being calculated. Drawing 1×1 Mechanical Tubing as a simple rectangle is fine for simple theatrical drafting, but it would be an inaccurate model to use for calculating the mass properties as mechanical tubing is hollow and has rounded corners.

When performing the Mass Properties command on 2D regions, the command will provide you with the area of the objects, the perimeter of the objects, the bounding box (or where the items exist on the X, Y, Z plane) and the centroid of the objects along the X, Y, Z plane of your AutoCAD window.

When performing the Mass Properties command on 3D solids, the command will provide you with all of the same information from above and also include values for the volume of the object, moments of inertia, the products of inertia, the radii of gyration and the principle moments and X, Y, Z directions about the centroid.

You will notice that the volume of objects are equal to the mass of the object as mass is set to a default value of one unit per unit of volume. The volume is set to match drawing units, meaning that if your drawing units are in inches, the volume of an object will be given in inches cubed. To calculate actual mass of an object, you will need to find mass per volume of a given material. For example, steel weighs approximately 0.29 pounds per cubic inch. Multiplying the volume provided for an object by 0.29 would give you the mass of that object if it were fabricated from steel.

While the calculations provided in the Mass Properties command in AutoCAD are accurate based on the geometry provided, it is always a good idea to consult a certified engineer when planning to construct structural assemblies.

While the Mass Properties command provides good information for basic engineering calculations, it is also worth noting that Autodesk has other software, such as Inventor and AutoCAD Mechanical, which have the ability to do far more with engineering than AutoCAD does.

Creating Custom Keyboard Shortcuts

While not a function of production or engineering, creating custom keyboard commands can save significant drafting time. I know many draftspersons who state that they perform the Copy command far more often than they draw circles, and therefore change the keyboard shortcut "C" to mean Copy instead of Circle and change Circle to something like "CI."

The definitions of which keyboard shortcuts access which commands in AutoCAD are held in a PGP file that is included with the software. These keyboard commands (called aliases) can be changed and customized, and aliases can be created to access commands by editing the PGP file.

To change the PGP file, navigate to the Express tab of the Ribbon in any of the three workspaces and click on the Command Aliases tool in the Tools panel of the Ribbon. The Alias Editor dialog box (Image 20.4) will load. From here you can add, remove and edit the aliases and their associated commands.

A list of aliases is on the left of the box with their associated AutoCAD commands on the right. To edit a command alias, highlight it on the left and click the Edit button. A new dialog box will load that will allow you to redefine what command should be associated with that alias. You can similarly create new aliases and associate those with AutoCAD commands.

References

Bell, Greg, et al. "USITT Scenic Design and Technical Production Drafting Standards." *Theatre Design and Technology*, 1999.

Dorn, D and Shanda, M. 2012. *Drafting for the Theatre*. Carbondale: Southern Illinois University Press.

Sohail, U. "What Is the Difference Between First and Third Angle Projection? A Mechanical Engineer Explains." *Wonderful Engineering*, 23 June 2017, wonderfulengineering.com/difference-first-third-angle-projection-mechanical-engineer-explains/.

Index

Align (AL) 50
Aligned Dimension (DAL) 104
Allow Exploding 63
Alternate Unit tab 103
American National Standards Institute (ANSI) 39
Animated Motion Path 158
Animation tools 159
Annotate panel 103
Annotation 12–13; tools 19, 154
Annotative *vs.* Standard dimensions 100–101
annual subscription 2
Arc (A) 35
Arc Length (DAR) 104
Arc subcommand 33
Array (AR) 51
Arrows tab 102
attach 85
Attach DWG 83
Attribute 69–70; definitions 69
Authoring Palettes 78
AutoCAD: annual subscription 2; creating account 4; downloading 4–5; educational license 2–3; installing 5–6; licenses 1; menu 16; migrating custom settings 6; monthly subscription 2; mouse necessity 3–4; note about processors 3; opening 6–7; perpetual license 1; registering license 6; system requirements 3; uninstalling and license transferring 7; vs. CAD for Mac 1
Auto Constrain command 76
Autodesk account 4
Axis, End 38

Baseline dimension 104–105
base points 62
Base Point subcommand 126
base view 150–151
bind 85
Block Attribute Manager (BATTMAN) 73

Block Authoring palette 78
Block Editor 64, 65
Block Manager 64
blocks: content 76; creating 62; dynamic 77; exploding 63; geometry 64; geometry of 76–77; inserting 63–64; mirroring 65; naming 62; nested 66; several 77; unit settings 63
Boolean tools 132
Box command 121
broken XREF links 86

CAD for Mac 1
camera: properties 155–157; views 156–158
CAMERA (CAM) 156
center 38
center grips 41–42
center point 34
chamfer (CHA) 37, 48–49
Chamfer Edges command 140
Check Solids command 141
Circle (C) 34
Clean Solids command 141
Close Block Editor 71
closed polyline 34
Close Test Block 72
Color Edge command 141
Color Face command 139
Command Line 15, 33
Computer-Aided Design (CAD) 8
Computer Numerical Control (CNC) 162–163
Cone (CONE) 122
Constraint Bar 75
constraints 74–76, 78
Construction Line (XL) 20–21, 38
continuous dimension 104–105
Copy (CO or CP) 43, 44, 165
Copy Edge command 140–141
Copy Face command 137, 164
Copy Faces method 164
copying layout 92–93
corner grips 42

Create Section Block tool 147–148
Crossing Selection 32
custom keyboard commands 165–166
Custom User Interface file (CUI) 26–27
Cylinder (CYL) 122

default method 36
Delete Face command 138
Design Center 161–162
detach 85
detail views 148, 153
Detail View Style Manager 153
Diameter Dimension tool (DIMDIA) 104
dimensions 31–32; Alternate Unit tab 103; Annotate panel 103; Annotative *vs.* Standard 100–101; association 105; continuous *vs.* baseline 104–105; Fit tab 103; Lines tab 102; modification 101; Primary Units tab 101–102; Quick 105; for rectangles 36–37; style 100; Symbols and Arrows tab 102; Text tab 102–103; Tolerance tab 103; types of 103–104
Dimension Style Manager 100–103
Display Alternate Dimension 103
Display tab 23–24
drafting commands 20–21, 30
Drafting tab 25
drawing tools 39
Drawing Units 22
Drawing View Editor tab 152
dynamic block 74, 77; steps for making 76
dynamic input 19

Edge Editing commands 139
edge grips 42
editing blocks 72
educational license 2–3
Ellipse (EL) 38
Enhanced Attribute Editor 72–73
entering text 68
Erase (E) 45, 46
ETRANSMIT 89–90
Explode (X) 47
Export Files 162
Extend (EX) 45–46
External Reference: binding 89; clipping 86–88; drawings with 88–89; ETRANSMIT 89–90; files 83–84; Manager 83; manipulation 86; shortcut menu 84–86
Extrude (EXT) command 124
Extrude Faces command 136

Face Editing command 135–136
fence selection 33
Field of View 158
File menu 23
Fillet (F) 37, 48, 49
Fillet Edges command 139–140
1st angle projection 11–12
Fit tab 103
Flatshot 148–149, 163–164
Free Hand Revision Cloud 108
Function bar 16, 19, 20

geometrical dimensioning and tolerance (GD&T) 13
geometric constraints 75
Gizmos 128–130
grid and grid snap 17
grips 41

Half Width subcommand 34
Hardware Acceleration 20
Hatch (H) 39
Helix (HELIX) 123–124
Help menu 16
hidden line 11
Hidden Line plot style 145
Hide Objects (HIDEOB) 59

importing files 162
Imprint command 135
Insert Field 70
inserting blocks 72
insertion point 71
installation 5–6
Interfere command 134–135
International Organization for Standards (ISO) 9
Intersect command 133
invert clip 87
Isolate Objects (ISOLATE) 59
isometric drafting 18

Join (J) 46

Lasso 32–33
layer 53, 54; color 55; drawing objects on 57–58; locking 57; moving objects between 57–58; names 54; plot 56–57; turning off *vs.* freezing 57; working with 57

Layer Isolate (LAYISO) 58–59
Layer Property Manager 53, 54, 57, 61
Layout: tabs 14, 15; *vs.* Model tab 91
layout 11; deleting 92; renaming 92; sheet 93
leaders 105–106
License Transfer Utility (LTU) 7
lighting 76
Lighting Instrument 77
Line (L) 31
Linear Dimension (DLI) 104
lines: of specified dimensions 31; type 10, 55–56; weight display 20; weights 10, 56
Lines tab 102
Loft command 127

Make Object's Layer Current 58
Mass Properties command 164–165
Match Layer Properties (MA) 58
Maximize Viewport 115
Menu Bar 22
Migrate Custom Settings 6
Mirror (MI) 43
miscellaneous layer options 59
modeling 113 *see also* 3D modeling
model space 14–15, 114; selection 17, 151; Viewport 115
Model tab 14
Model Views 158
modes 70–71
modify panel 147
monthly subscription 2
Motion Path Animation 159
mouse necessity 3–4
Move (M) 42–43
Move Faces command 137
moving layout 92–93
multileader (MLD) 105–106
Multileader Style Manager 106
Multiline text (MTEXT) 67
Multiple subcommand (M) 125

Navigation Bar 116–117
Nested Copy (NCOPY) 66
New Layout tab 92
nonsymmetrical chamfers 49

Object Grips 32, 33, 157
objects: dimensions 31–32; with grips 41; properties 59–60; selection 32, 62, 63; snap 18–19
Offset (O) 47–48
Offset Faces command 138

open 84
opening *vs.* loading templates 28–29
Open tab 24
OPTIONS 22–23
Orbit *see* 3D Orbit (3DO) command
Orbit command 158
Ordinate Dimensions 104
origin grips 119–120
orthogonal 17–18
orthographic mode 119
OSNAPS 130
Overkill (OV) 46–47

Page Setup Manager 93–94
paper sizes 8–9, 95
parameters 78
path 158–159; array 52
perpetual license 1
plot: layers 56–57; menu 109; options 97; orientation 97
Plot Area 95
Plot Style Tables (Pen Assignments) 95–97
plotter selection 95
Point commands 128
polar array 51–52
Polar Array option 131
polar snap modes 17–18
Polar Tracking Mode 119
polygon (POL) 37–38, 87
Polygonal Revision Cloud 108
Polyline (PL) 33, 87
Poly Solid (POLYSOLID) 123
Press-Pull command 125
previous button 58
Primary Units tab 101–102
processors 3
projected views 151
Properties Manager 59–60
Publishing Layouts 110–111
Purge (PU) 66
Pyramid (PYR) 122

Quick access toolbar 16, 45
quick dimensions 105
Quick Leader (QL) 105–106

radius 34
Radius Dimension tool (DIMRAD) 104
Recent Blocks 63
Rectangle (REC) 36
rectangular 87
rectangular array 51
Redo 45

Refedit toolbar 64–65
reference angles 44
reference lines 10, 72
Regenerate (RE) 40
registering license 6
reload 85
Repeat last command 36
Revision Cloud 107–108
Revolve command 126–127
Ribbon 21
right-click menu 91
rotate 44
Rotate (RO) 44
Rotate 3D command 130
Rotate Face command 138–139
Rotate Gizmo 157
rotate parameter 80–81

Save tab 24
Saving blocks 71
Scale (SC) 49–50
scale factors 130
Scale Gizmo 130
SECTION (SEC) 145–146
Section Plane 146–148
SECTIONPLANESETTINGS 147
section views 12, 152
Section View Style Modification
    dialog box 152–153
selection cycling 19
Selection tab 25–26
select polyline 87
Select the Lithography (STL) file
    format 164
Separate Solids command 141
shapes 37–38
Sheet layouts: plotting 109–110;
    publishing 110–111
Shell command 141–142
Shortcut menu 43, 45
Slice command 133–134
Smart Dimension tool (DIM) 104
Solid Editing commands 113,
    132–142
Sphere (SPH) 122
Standard vs. annotative text 68
Start, Center, End 35
Start, Center, Length 35–36
Start, End, Radius 35
Steering Wheel 116
Stretch (S) 42
Subtract command 133
Sweep command 125–126
Symbols tab 102
system requirements 3

Table Styles 107
Table tool 106–107
Tangent, Tangent, Radius 35
Taper Face command 137
template 27–28
test and save 81–82
Test Block 71–72
text 67; settings 71; styles 67–68; tab
    102–103
3rd angle projection 11–12
3D modeling 112–127; drafting
    primitive 3D shapes 121–124;
    Extrude command 124–127;
    plating 143–154
3D model space, 112–127;
    navigation bar 116–117; orbit
    114; solid editing 113; setting up
    112–113; steering wheel 116; UCS
    command 118–120; view controls
    117; view cube 116; viewing 113;
    view options within 114; viewport
    configuration 115; viewport
    controls 115; view toolbar 114;
    visual styles controls 117
3D Move Gizmo 157
3D object: Gizmos 128–129; Point
    commands 128; Rotate 3D
    command 130; scale factors 130;
    snap 20; 3D Align command 131;
    3D Array 131; 3D Mirror 130–131;
    3D Move 129; 3D Rotate 129–130
3D Orbit (3DO) command 114
3DORBITCTR 114
3D printers 164
three-point method 34, 35
Title blocks 9, 68–69
Tolerance tab 103
Tool palettes 53–54
Torus 123
transparency 20, 56
Trim (TR) 45–46
Turning off vs. freezing layers 57
Turning On/Off Xclips 87
two-dimensional drafting 154
2D Polyline Selection (PEDIT) 46
2D shape 124
two-point method 35

UCS see User Coordinate System
    (UCS)
UCSICON 119
Undo 45, 46
Undo Polyline command 34
uninstalling 7
Union command 132–133

Unisolate Layers button 58–59
United States Institute of Theatre
    Technology (USITT) 8
unload 85
User Coordinate System (UCS)
    112, 121; command 118; Face
    command 118; manipulating
    118; moving, using origin grips
    119–120; Object command 118;
    origin, saved custom 120; rotating
    118; 3 Points command 119; World
    command 119
User Preferences tab 24–25

View 113
View Base command 149–151
view cube 116
View Manager 158
Viewport 97–98, 158; activating 98;
    configuration 115; controls 115,
    117; multiple 98; plating using
    143–145; scaling and locking
    98–99

VIEWPORTS 115
View toolbar 114
visibility states 78–80
Visual Effect Settings toolbox 26
Visual Styles Controls 117

Walk and Fly Settings 160
W Blocks 88
Wedge (WEDGE) 122–123
Width subcommand 34
Window Selection 32
Wipeout 107–108
Workspace settings 19
Workspaces options 26
"World" UCS position 118

XREF: links 86; paths 85–86; type 85

Zoom (Z) 39–40
ZOOMWHEEL 39